Napoleon's Chicken

Recipes Fit for Emperors;
Designed for Weekend Cooks.

Bob Cotten

South on a Plate Books

South on a Plate
Publications

For Judy, Robert and Anne

Cover design by South on a Plate.

Interior design and formatting by Vanessa Hoffpauir.

Contents

CAUTION:
Read this First!

Originally, this book was supposed to be a collection of my old newspaper columns from "The Bachelor Cook". However, I found that I couldn't go back and enjoy patching all that stuff back together. It was boring.

I am greatly indebted to Wall Street Journal columnist, Eric Felten, whose book *"How's Your Drink? Cocktails, Culture, and the Art of Drinking Well"** showed me the way to do what I wanted to do all along which was to make a book not just about recipes or food, but also about some of the fascinating stories behind them.

So this is a book for reading as well as for cooking and I hope you will use it to enjoy doing both of those things was well as greatly pleasing your fortunate dinner guests.

– Bob Cotten, 2011

**Surrey Books, an Agate Imprint, Chicago, 2007*

Introduction

Prometheus Carrying Fire - Jan Cossiers

"Pop the cork, let's do supper"

Paleontologists virtually define prehistoric humanity as becoming human on the evidence that somebody was cooking something. Oyster shells dug from beds of charcoal along with various animal bones are key indicators that our ancestors had crossed the line from eating roots, berries and raw fish to feasting on good old smoky barbecue and shish kebabs.

The human pleasures derived from hunting and gathering and gathering and cooking originated probably not very long after the first use of fire by people around a million and a half years ago. Neanderthal remnants in French caves indicate that cooking had reached such an advanced level some 100,000 years before Julia Child that people were cooking large animals inside their skins with fire-heated stones and making broth possibly to keep alive crippled or toothless members who couldn't fend for themselves.

The early Greeks credited the Titan god, Prometheus, with stealing fire from heaven and giving it to humans. Thus began our long romance with heat-treated food which crafty gourmands have articulated through the slow roll of the millennia into such worthy dishes as veal marsala with mushrooms, green curry shrimp and chicken Marengo.

It was my undeserved good fortune to live in a rented beach house on Florida's east coast one year. We could barely afford beer sometimes but on weekends a group of us would fish in the surf or the salt marsh to catch our supper. Thus we made up for in fun what we lacked in the ability to eat out.

Those were memorable evenings. We'd cook speckled trout, court bouillon, oyster pudding or fried redfish, drink cold martinis or gin and tonic. Those who didn't want to cut onions or make stock could play guitar, bartend or run up the road for more ice. We all got involved, even the kids, who couldn't seem to resist hanging out in the kitchen listening to the grown ups.

On those balmy nights at the beach house, watching the moon on the ocean and hearing the surf, it was easy to imagine people doing something quite similar a quarter-million years ago.

Same moon. Same sound.

And, with the exception of a few dry martinis, the same convivial pleasures.

Foods have stories

Many of the dishes we enjoy today were also enjoyed by people who made history or by events which became history. Some of the stories behind the foods involved are fascinating and can enhance the enjoyment of gatherings around the dinner table.

Montezuma drank a mixture of unsweetened chocolate, corn flour and chile peppers which the Aztecs considered sacred but which you and I almost certainly would not. "Papa" Hemingway lent his expertise and his nickname to the "Papa Doble," an unsweetened daiquiri which has become legendary and is represented in this book. Napoleon so loved his chef's battlefield chicken dish that he ordered it served after every subsequent battle. That's in here, too. Good foods are delights in the present, many of which we receive as gifts from the past.

"Same moon. Same sound"

"Bear in mind that you should conduct yourself in life as at a feast."

– Epictetus

Comments About the Plans

The level of difficulty is greatly reduced for any plan simply by taking the time to organize the stuff you're going to use.

First step: Arrange a space or two on your counter tops and clear the junk off. You will work best in a clean and cleared space.

Second step: Get out all the things you will use, starting with the tools and then the ingredients. Center this around your cutting board. *(Each plan will tell you what these things are).*

Little bowls: These are a great help. Just marshall the prepped ingredients you'll use into separate little bowls, ready to toss in as needed.

Walnut-sized glob: Typically a mounded spoonful. You can use a tablespoon if you want to.

Handful: The maximum amount of dry stuff that you can hold in one hand cupped. A small handful is a mound of dry stuff in your palm.

Coffee mug or measuring cup: Either way, it's a "unit." Just keep the same unit throughout.

Tablespoon: Typically, the big spoon you find in the kitchen drawer or else the biggest of those big spoons on the ring.

You can add but you can't subtract: You can tweak something by adding a little at a time if necessary but once the salt or Tabasco or whatever is in the mix you can't get it back out.

Chop versus slice: You chop by first cutting strips and then cutting the strips across at a right angle. You slice by cutting strips to the thickness you want and leaving it at that.

Your knife: If you don't already have a cook's knife or chef's knife you really, *really* ought to invest in one. Get a honing "steel" to go with it to keep its edge effective. Every time, just before you use a knife, run each edge along the steel 15 times at a 30 degree angle.

Do this every time! That way your cutting edge will work for you not against you and will make your efforts on the cutting board a lot easier. Make this a routine.

Using a steel will not sharpen the blade but it will realign the microscopic deformities that happen each time the blade is used and will make it feel sharper and actually cut better.

You might want to sharpen your blade every year or so by grinding a new edge on a honing block which you should be able to get at a good hardware store. Put the honing block on a wet dish towel on a counter (to keep it from sliding) and firmly move the blade across it like you were trying to "shave" the block. Put some honing oil (or olive oil) on the block.

Disclaimer: The products identified in the plans which follow are things that I am partial to. I specify them because I have tried them over many years and they give you consistent, good results.

NOTE: *Each plan in here lists the tools that you will need to make it.*

"THOMAS JEFFERSON"
BY REMBRANDT PEALE

RECIPES & STORIES

"Eat Your Eggplant!"
THIRD PRESIDENT, FIRST EGGPLANT

MR. JEFFERSON'S GARDEN; AMERICAN ORIGIN OF "SOLANUM MELONGENA"

KID STUFF

If you look back on the things you liked as a kid and compare it to the things you like now, you will notice some interesting contrasts. For example, any normal, seven-year old male, given a choice of spending time naked in a hot tub with a centerfold model or with a live turtle in a sand box will go for the turtle reflexively.

To your seven-year old taste buds, a sip of your Dad's beer made you wonder what in the world he could have thought good about it. A dozen years later, motivated by a consuming thirst and a young sophomore's fully developed recreational inclination, you were buying kegs of it to guzzle at weekend parties.

As you get older you can't help but observe the phenomenon of bad stuff turning good by the simple interweaving of a few years.

This applies especially to food.

Goodbye to a cherished food foe

I once thought I would never live long enough to like eggplant. I also thought the same thing about beer.

Nothing my mother ever did to eggplant made it taste like food. Sorry, it just didn't make the cut.

The only thing more offensive than eggplant was rutabaga and because I would not allow myself a second experience with it, rutabaga never got classified as "food" at all. Rutabagas were a form of culinary abuse. Nobody had any business eating rutabagas.

Many years later, I enjoyed some eggplant at a backyard party without knowing what it was. It had shrimp in it. It was good enough to go back for seconds.

"What is this casserole?" I asked.

"Why, that's my shrimp and eggplant," answered my gracious hostess, thus bringing to an end another long-held food prejudice.

Eggplant probably was in use as long ago as 2,000 BC, by people in the region of south Asia which includes China and Burma. It didn't reach American shores until the Spaniards unloaded some in Florida in the early 1600's. However, it remained undiscovered by what later became known as Americans until Thomas Jefferson planted some in his garden at Monticello around 1806.

But Jefferson only ate it after he grew up

You could be forgiven for wondering if there was anything Jefferson *didn't* get around to doing. When he wasn't inventing machines or representing his country in Europe, writing the Declaration of Independence or building a university, he was busy raising well over 200 varieties of fruits and vegetables in an incredible garden which he designed and from which he supplied his family and guests throughout much of the year.

Apparently, he had enjoyed *"roasted eggplant with garlic and sesame seeds"* while serving as a diplomat to the French court in 1784, and brought some eggplant seeds home for this garden.

SHRIMP & EGGPLANT

The tools:

- Cutting board
- Cook's knife
- Garlic press
- 4-quart pot with lid
- 3-quart baking dish
- Colander
- 3 or 4-quart bowl
- Measuring spoons

Here's what you need from the store:
(See note below)

- One pound raw shrimp
- One large eggplant (or two small)
- One tennis ball sized onion
- Grated Romano cheese
- Grated mild yellow cheddar cheese
- Chicken base paste *(see page 4)*
- Extra large (or jumbo) eggs
- Unsalted butter
- Unseasoned, fine bread crumbs
  (Rienzi makes a dependable product)
- Black pepper
- Cayenne pepper
- Paprika

(Note: Your initial costs for the dry stuff, the chicken base and the eggs, etc. obviously will not be lost by being totally used up and thus you can apply these things to subsequent plans.)

Here's how you put it together:

1. Set your oven to bake at 350 degrees.

2. Cut the eggplant into 1-inch cubes.

3. Put this in a pot with just enough water to cover and cook on medium heat for 20 minutes while you peel & chop the onion and peel the shrimp.

4. Drain the cooked eggplant in the colander with the bowl underneath and reserve about a quarter cupful of the cooking water. Throw the rest of it out.

5. Put the cooked eggplant into the bowl and add the finely chopped onions, a stick of butter, the raw shrimp, a walnut-sized gob of chicken base paste, 5 eggs, a half cup or mug of finely grated Romano cheese, some black pepper, some cayenne (red pepper) and a quarter-cup of the fine bread crumbs. Stir all this to mix well.

6. Pour this mixture into the baking dish and sprinkle some of the Romano cheese on the top. Garnish with paprika sprinkled around the outside of the top.

7. Bake for 50 minutes. Allow to cool and "set" for 15 minutes. Serve hot.

A likely first encounter

While he was president, Jefferson set a welcome table for visitors to the White House, frequently hosting members of the House and Senate as well as foreign dignitaries and Cherokee Indian chiefs.

With his French Chef, Julien, in charge, the dinners were lavish but, as specified by Jefferson himself, "never wasteful." Three such dinners occurred each week, with the remainder of the week's evening meals shared with family and friends.

Jefferson did little talking at these events but rather employed himself in personally serving his guests' plates and making sure they had no want at his table.

Amazing: the President of the country actually served the food from the platter to the plates of his guests! Such behavior is the mark of a genuinely secure man.

After designing and founding the University of Virginia, he made sure that one of the subjects taught in its classrooms was Italian, which he spoke fluently, along with French, and which greatly facilitated his voracious curiosity during his travels in Italy.

I am guessing that the eggplant Jefferson enjoyed in France might well have been the Mediterranean dish we know as ratatouille or something similar. It is a melange of vegetables which, you will find, can be adapted for a variety of tastes. In India, for example, it is cooked with curry pastes and with various fiery chiles in Thailand.

JEFFERSON SERVED AS MINISTER TO FRANCE FROM 1784 TO 1789 AND TENDED A SMALL VEGETABLE GARDEN ADJACENT TO HIS HOUSE. HE MADE FRENCH TARRAGON VINEGAR AND BROUGHT TARRAGON SEEDS HOME BEFORE BEING ELECTED PRESIDENT IN 1800.

Replace the salt with flavor

Purists may turn their noses up at the idea of using meat base pastes but you shouldn't. I routinely use chicken base paste *as the replacement for salt* and find that it adds an unbeatable richness to whatever I make. *You don't need to blend it with water first.* Just add it directly to the other ingredients, including water. Be sure that, whatever brand you buy, salt is **NOT** the first listed ingredient on the label.

"You want Jefferson Fries with that?"

At the age of nine, you don't know who to blame for eggplant. But when you get a little older and you start to like it, it adds a measure of historical cachet to know that it was Thomas Jefferson himself; inventor of the swivel chair, the dual polygraph, the code-cipher machine, the Lewis and Clark Expedition, much of the Declaration of Independence and the first famous American aficionado of fine French wine.

It was Thomas Jefferson who brought home from southern France the nation's first pasta machine and thus started our love affair with macaroni and cheese.

Moreover, it was Jefferson, a man who died in debt, who was responsible for the Louisiana Purchase which ultimately gave America the French Quarter thereby bequeathing to posterity such priceless American treasures as eggs Sardou and the oyster po-boy.

Among Jefferson's many contributions to carpentry, horticulture, government, philosophy, writing and politics, you should note as well those in the culinary arts, including the introduction to America of French fries and eggplant and the spread of the popularity of ice cream. If you stripped away all his other talents and accomplishments, you'd still have a world-class foodie. Fried potato strips appeared on European tables as early as 1680, although the French fry as we know it is claimed by Belgium and Spain as well as France. Nobody calls them Spanish fries or Belgian fries, however. Jefferson referred to them as *"potatoes fried in deep fat while raw, first having been cut into small slices."*

How's that for succinct?

You can imagine that Jefferson, a reserved man in politics and manners, might have been a real hoot to cook with in his own kitchen, even if he weren't actually stirring the pot but merely leaning against a table sipping a Bordeaux and holding forth on clocks, dumb-waiters, Architecture, wine, celestial navigation, astronomy, diplomacy, the pruning of fruit trees, the pacifying of Indian tribes, the evolution of language, the science of navigation and the perils of big government.

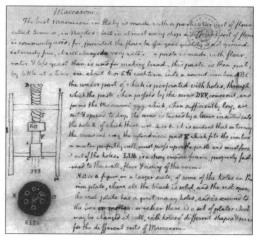

JEFFERSON'S DRAWING OF HIS PASTA MACHINE

It is likely that he would have encountered *"potatoes, fried in deep fat while raw, first having been cut into small pieces"* on numerous occasions around Paris. What a relief it must have been years later to just call them French fries.

French fried potatoes are not easy to make in your kitchen and I strongly recommend that you don't try it without investing in your own, personal fire engine. Moreover, there is an art to making really good French Fries which involves techniques requiring considerable prep time.

But you *can* french-fry peeled eggplant to great effect. The slices cook up crisp on the outside and tender on the inside and you can probably do it with nothing more elaborate on hand than a single fire extinguisher.

FRENCH-FRIED EGGPLANT

Peel the eggplant and slice it across, with the slices being about an inch thick. Quarter the slices so that you end up with a bunch of more or less rounded-end triangles. Then season these with salt, black pepper and/or cayenne pepper and shake them in flour in a Ziplock bag and fry in peanut oil that is about an inch deep. Get the oil hot — ideally you want about 400 degrees — then carefully lay the cut-up pieces into the oil. Lay them in with something that has a long handle so that you won't get burned. Remove with a slotted spoon quickly as soon as they turn golden in color, drain on paper towels and serve immediately.

FRENCH-FRIED EGGPLANT

RATATOUILLE AT THE TABLE

The tools:

- Cutting board
- 3 bowls
- Cook's knife
- Garlic press
- Large skillet with a lid (or Dutch oven)

Here's what you need from the store:

- Garlic
- Olive oil*
- Dried Greek oregano
- 1 small to medium-sized fresh zucchini
- 2 large jalapeno chile peppers
- 1 small red bell pepper
- A medium eggplant
- Chicken base paste
- Fresh parsley
- Fresh basil
- Black pepper
- A couple of tennis ball sized tomatoes
- French bread
- Sesame seeds

Note: Whenever olive oil is used in any of these plans, it should be understood that is "extra virgin."

Here's how you put it together:

1. Chop the eggplant into 1/2-inch or 1-inch cubes and set aside.
2. Chop 2 seeded jalapenos and 1 seeded red bell pepper into quarter-inch pieces and put them in a separate bowl.
3. Chop the zucchini into 1-inch cubes and put them in a separate bowl.
4. Smash the garlic or finely chop it and put it in the skillet, on medium heat, with some olive oil.
5. Chop the onion and add it to the skillet. Cook for 6 minutes.
6. Add the eggplant, stir it in.
7. Add the chopped red bell pepper and the chopped jalapenos.
8. Cover the skillet and cook this for about 10 more minutes. (stir a couple of times to make sure nothing is sticking to the bottom.)
9. Add 2 or 3 tomatoes cut into eighths.
10. Add a spoonful of chicken base paste to replace the salt and add flavor.
11. Add the cut up zucchini and then some dried Greek oregano, a small handful of chopped fresh basil, a small handful of chopped fresh parsley and some black pepper.
12. With heat on low, cover the skillet and allow to cook for about 15 minutes.
13. Serve hot or cold with toasted French bread, dipped in olive oil, and coated with toasted sesame seeds.

It is a well established fact that Jefferson almost never dined alone. Meals were an opportunity for lively discussion (politics usually not included) and the social pleasures of exploring ideas through dialogue. Jefferson's dining table was round in order to facilitate the social nature of enjoying delightful meals.

"Mr. Doodle WAS a Macaroni"

In late 17th Century Italy, it became the habit of certain foppish young men to draw attention to themselves by wearing outlandish clothes and extremely tall wigs. These dandies were called "macaroni" in Italy and travelers there picked up the term and brought it back. Young Englishmen copied this fashion as a means of showing off their elite status as worldly and well-travelled.

In his book, *The Life of Dr. Johnson*, James Boswell reports seeing the ungainly Johnson on horseback while touring the Hebrides with him and of telling him; "you are a delicate Londoner; you are a macaroni; you can't ride."

When Yankee Doodle "stuck a feather in his cap and called it macaroni," that is exactly what the term was referring to; the outlandish dandies of Italy and England; the "macaroni" with their ridiculously high wigs.

Before the Revolutionary War, some snooty Englishmen referred to American colonists as "yankee doodles," doodle being a derisive term which meant "simpleton." However, the Americans had a sense of ironic humor and took the little ditty as a favorite all the way to the surrender of the British at Yorktown, in 1781.

Jefferson's Monticello Macaroni

Jefferson encountered the kind of macaroni that goes on a plate near the Mediterranean in 1787. He fell in love with it and devised a machine for making macaroni noodles which he constructed at Monticello.

But the cooks in his kitchen may never have routinely used it, preferring instead to simply roll the pasta by hand on small diameter dowels. The following plan is the way macaroni was prepared in Monticello's kitchen.

A "MACARONI": LONDON, 1774

MONTICELLO'S PARMESAN MACARONI

(This is tastier than the macaroni most of us are used to! • Serves 6)

The tools:

- Pot for boiling water
- Large skillet or Dutch oven
- Colander for straining noodles
- Oven-proof baking dish
- Whisk

Here's what you need from the store:

- 1 pound box of macaroni noodles
- 3 - 8 oz. packs grated Parmesan cheese (Parmesan replaces salt)
- Black pepper
- Unsalted butter
- Unseasoned fine bread crumbs
- Paprika

Here's how you put it together:

1. Melt a half-stick of butter in a very large skillet or Dutch oven.
2. Put 2 cups full of macaroni noodles into a big pot of unsalted boiling water.
3. Mix a quarter cupful of flour into the butter until smooth then slowly whisk in 2 cupfuls of milk, stirring constantly with the whisk.
4. When this mixture is thick and smooth add the cooked noodles and blend.
5. Add 2 cups grated Parmesan cheese and stir it in completely.
6. Add some black pepper. You can use a lot.
7. Pour this mixture into a greased, 2-quart baking dish.
8. Sprinkle more Parmesan cheese and some bread crumbs over the top.
9. Cut some butter and drop small bits across the top.
10. Garnish with paprika sprinkled around the edges.
11. Bake at 350 degrees for 25 minutes.

Sweet Potatoes "Thomas Jefferson"

Serves 6

The tools:
- Cutting board
- Cook's knife
- 2-quart baking dish
- Potato masher
  (you can also just use a fork)
- 2-quart bowl

Here's what you need from the store:
- 2 large, red, sweet potatoes
- Seedless tangerines
- Brown sugar
- Butter
- Cinnamon
- "Baby" marshmallows (optional)

Here's how you put it together:

1. Boil sweet potatoes until tender (or microwave the two for 16 minutes total).

2. When cool, peel and mash in a bowl.

3. Add one-third stick of butter and a very little bit of salt.

4. Add some brown sugar (maybe a walnut-sized mound).

5. Squeeze in the juice of half a sweet tangerine.

6. Tap in a light "dusting" of cinnamon and mash all this together, blending well.

7. Put this into a baking dish.

8. Top with marshmallows if desired and bake at 350 degrees for 30 minutes.

Jefferson's garden included more vegetables than most family farms but records from Monticello indicate some preferences, such as various cabbages, tomatoes, beans and peas.

Interestingly, Jefferson purchased a variety of vegetables for his household from the slaves on his 5,000 acre plantation. These people had their own garden plots and cultivated an entirely separate money economy for themselves by selling the produce they grew to Jefferson and to other families nearby.

Thomas Jefferson more or less started the French wine craze in America and was known in his day as the country's foremost wine expert. He popularized ice cream and featured numerous dishes from the fruits of his own property as fine as those in Paris at the time.

"I have lived temperately, eating little animal food and that as a condiment for the vegetables which constitute my principal diet."

– Thomas Jefferson, Monticello, 1819
The year he founded the University of Virginia

Did you Know?

Marshmallow sweets were eaten in ancient Egypt. This was a honey-flavored candy that was thickened with the sap of the marsh mallow plant, indigenous to salt marshes and the banks of big rivers and lakes. It is also common to the eastern part of the U.S., from whence Jefferson's cooks may have obtained it. French confectioners were making marshmallow based candies by the mid 1800s. Today, gelatin replaces the sap.

MARSH MALLOW PLANT
CREDIT: TWISTEDCANDY.COM

"Christopher Columbus" by Carl von Piloty

The Fruits of Conquest

"COLUMBUS TAKING POSSESSION OF THE NEW COUNTRY"
PRANG & CO.; U.S. LIBRARY OF CONGRESS, LC-USZC2-1687

"ADMIRAL OF THE OCEAN SEA"

Imagine that it is around midnight, September 5, 1492. In your entire world there is no tobacco, bourbon, penicillin, insect repellent, kerosene or rubber. There is no ice, no radio. Pizza and electricity have not been invented. There won't be any clocks for another 165 years and you are on a small wooden ship a few hundred miles out on a very dark ocean.

Imagine that you are Christopher Columbus, standing on the high weather deck of the little ship you have commanded since leaving Spain a few days ago. There is no radar, no Coast Guard, the barometer is 152 years away from being invented and you don't know that it is hurricane season in the Atlantic.

You hear the ship creak as it rolls beneath your legs, confidently splitting the sea. Above you shines a dome of bright stars, some swaying in and out behind the square foresail. You stare ahead, to the west, your eyes drifting from the sky to the foaming water below and the phosphorescence caused by dolphins ahead of the bow. To the west! You're going west!

Everybody knows you get to China and India in the other direction. But you, no, you are Columbus! You are certain that you can get there going this way. It is insane! They called you crazy, didn't they? Were they right? Do you begin to entertain doubts? Anyway, it's too late to go back now and there is no GPS. Good grief – you won't even be able to call home for another 503 years!

Columbus was wrong!

And a good thing, too, for Columbus and his crew.

He was right to know that if you sailed westward you would eventually reach the orient because everybody in educated society knew the world was a sphere. In Alexandria, the Greek mathematician Eratosthenes had correctly estimated the circumference to within a few miles in 240 BC.

However, Columbus, lacking Eratosthenes' empirical geometry, was wrong about the size of the sphere! He used an incorrect measure for land miles and then transposed that to nautical miles!

Therefore he badly miscalculated the distance of a degree on the world sphere and thus the distance from Spain to Asia by about two and a half times, leaving out the whole north American landmass and the entire expanse of the Pacific Ocean. His calculations told him he could get to India within 30 days because it had to be only 2,400 miles from Spain!

No fully manned sailing vessel at the time had room enough to carry the amount of food and water required for a voyage of more than about 30 days.

It is amazing that Columbus's huge error nonetheless correctly estimated the distance which he actually did traverse and got him safely to shore. Think about that . . . You stake your life on an "educated" guess that turns out to be wrong by two orders of magnitude and then wind up in a place that nobody in your world has ever heard of and suddenly you're an overnight sensation!

Mind you, this voyage was not like sailing around the coast of Africa; you couldn't send the oarboat ashore from time to time for fresh water and wild game. A couple-dozen days out would put Columbus past the point of no return! His great gamble paid off precisely because he was wrong about the facts.

Had Columbus not been so drastically wrong in his calculations, it must be admitted that he, his ships and men might just as well have 'fallen off the face of the earth."

IT AIN'T CUISINE AND IT AIN'T HAUTE, BUT IT'LL EAT!

Food at sea in a wooden hulled vessel without ice is easily and quickly spoiled. You take stuff that can resist mold, such as dried meats and fish or salt-brined meat along with dried fruits, like raisins, and dried vegetables or nuts or things such as dried chick peas, almonds and rice. You take wine. If you bring any bread on board, you eat it within the first few days, before it grows a coating of green mold.

Provisions for Columbus and his men likely would have included cheese, honey, garlic, rice, salted sardines packed in wooden barrels, dehydrated, salted anchovies, salt pork, salt cod, molasses, hard cheese, and hard biscuits that you had to soak before eating. It would keep you alive and also make you a fine candidate for scurvy after eating nothing else for a month or so.

You can recreate an imagined crew's mess aboard one of Columbus's ships, using just the stuff those guys were likely to have on board. It is nondescript, as you may imagine, but it's hearty. The reason it is here is to provide a reasonable facsimile of a mariner's meal at sea in 1492, not to compete for any food award. If you don't serve it to guests you might find it to be an excellent lesson for the kids and also provide a platform for a little story-telling. You won't find it on anybody's menu.

"SANTA MARIA" STEW

The tools:
- Big skillet or pot that has a lid
- Big fork for turning
- Cutting board
- Cook's knife

Here's what you need from the store:
- Beef roast (5 or 6 pounds)
- Salt
- Onions
- Raisins
- Vinegar
- Olive oil
- Carrots
- Dried bay leaves
- Black pepper
- 2 cans chickpeas (garbanzos)

Here's how you put it together:

1. Soak the meat 10-12 hours in water to cover with 2 cups salt.
2. Next day, drain and brown the meat on all sides in olive oil.
3. Turn heat to medium-low.
4. Add 7-8 carrots (halved or sliced to 1" lengths).
5. Add 3 onions, cut into eighths.
6. Add 2 cans of chickpeas.
7. Add 3 handfuls of raisins plus as much black pepper as you like.
8. Pour in some olive oil, cover the pan, simmer about 5 hours.

Of course, Columbus and the boys did not have potatoes, chile peppers, tomatoes, beans, or corn to add to this. They probably didn't fare too badly, however, since whoever did the cooking was under a good deal of pressure to make the food as good-tasting as possible, or else suffer the wrath of disgruntled deckhands. Such was life aboard the Santa Maria.

If you do try making this I suggest separating the cooked meat with a large spoon and tongs into small pieces, mixing bits of the meat with the vegetables and raisins and chick peas and spooning this over crumbled, hot baguettes or toasted French bread slices.

There were drawbacks to making decent hot food on a ship at sea in 1492, not the least of them being the lack of a stove. Your supper was made over a fire on deck which had a windbreak to protect it. Sand was placed under the fire to keep the ship from burning. There was no saloon. The men took food from a large, common pot or kettle, each with his own knife. Fish or perhaps the occasional sea turtle would have been the sole source of fresh protein. Following is an example:

Tuna, medium-well if you please

On an old wooden schooner in the Atlantic many years ago, our cook caught a bluefin tuna of about 16 pounds by trolling a hand line off the stern. This would have been essentially the same equipment available to Columbus and his own cook.

The fillets were roughly six pounds each and he baked these on a bed of rice, cream sauce and mushrooms in large oven trays and served them with fried mushrooms and nicely caramelized onions.

Tuna aficionados who eat it nearly raw nowadays would look down their noses at such a thing but I assure you that it greatly pleased all the souls on that little voyage. He caught another one a few days later and everybody applauded (literally, clapping their hands) and could hardly wait for supper.

ABOARD THE "BEL ESPOIR" ON AN AUGUST AFTERNOON. FORWARD HATCH IN THE FOREGROUND.

The Santa Maria was Columbus's flagship and, for its day, was a worthy vessel. However, it was worthy only if you were sailing between established ports and weren't worried about running aground. It had a deep draft and became stuck on a reef off the island of what is now Haiti on Christmas Day, 1492. Columbus ordered the ship disassembled and used its timbers to construct a fortress at a place he named La Navidad on the island. It was the first Spanish settlement in the new world.

Millennium Herald

The night sky Columbus saw from the deck of his ship would have been full of significance for him. He wrote out his name as "Christoferens" which means "Christbearer" because he saw himself as God's messenger, in sync with cosmic events. He would save the lost souls of the east indies by bringing them into the fold of Christianity. As it turned out he was not only a lousy messenger but a formidably awful evangelizer.

Part of this conceit came from the sky – from a looming "conjunction" of Saturn and Jupiter. This is an event which occurs every 18 to 20 years in one of the 30 degree "houses" of the Zodiac, in such a way that the whole thing rotates back around to the starting point of the Zodiacal circle in 960 years. Astrologers said this 960-year cycle foretold of the end of one world age and the start of the next (and which is the basis for our concept of "millennium").

Columbus believed them, saw himself as on a mission from God, and hoped to complete that mission before Saturn and Jupiter made their big, celestial, cycle-restarting rendezvous.

Little did he know that it would be the *actual* events, not the star-crossed ones, which would see the end of one world and the beginning of another.

Did you Know?

The conjunctions of Saturn and Jupiter occur in the "houses" of the Zodiac (the twelve, 30-degree sections of sky which girdle the planet). After each alignment, they move apart and rejoin at the next conjunction roughly 118 degrees farther along the "wheel." These conjunctions occur 40 times to complete the cycle and thus start a new "millennium."

If you want to learn more about the connection between mythology and early astronomy, I cannot suggest a more fascinating, scientifically based book than "Hamlet's Mill: An Essay Investigating the

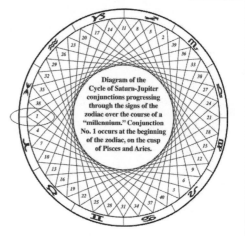

Diagram of the Cycle of Saturn-Jupiter conjunctions progressing through the signs of the zodiac over the course of a "millennium." Conjunction No. 1 occurs at the beginning of the zodiac, on the cusp of Pisces and Aries.

Origins of Human Knowledge and Its Transmission Through Myth" by Giorgio de Santillana and Hertha von Dechen.

The spice trade heats up

Spices in the 15th Century, especially black pepper, were worth their weight in gold and Columbus, apart from evangelizing lost heathens, sought a major coup against rival trading empires, especially Portugal. He would save the markets of Europe from the tyranny of the Ottomans* and beat the Portuguese in the bargain.

It seems amusing now that the India, Japan, and China, Columbus thought he discovered actually were land masses in the Caribbean, populated by naked people with a very relaxed lifestyle who did not, had Columbus cared to notice, look very much like Asians.

Columbus saw what he had for years prepared himself to see, replacing reality with an expectation. Many are thus lured into an abyss of their own manufacture.

Expectation is experienced as a kind of certainty, as may have been the case with Columbus, beyond which it becomes virtually impossible to perceive what is real.

Nor could the "Admiral of the Ocean Sea" have known that the "pepper" he found in his "Indies" were chiles, not *piper nigrum* or black pepper that Europeans so highly valued. So valued in fact, that it was sold by the individual peppercorn and people used it to pay their rents. Chiles, in their many varieties, were to become one of the single biggest discoveries of Columbus's and of Spain's entire expedition.

The seasoning of history

Columbus made four voyages to the New World, undoubtably never realizing that one major result would be a huge, worldwide demand for some amazing new foods.

These foods gave Europeans a millennial shift in culinary choices: potatoes, tomatoes, squash, beans of every variety, avocados, corn, chocolate, sweet potatoes (yams), vanilla and peanuts among others.

Think about it! No one in the whole of Europe or Asia, north of the Equator, had ever experienced these foods before 1492! Moreover, nobody in Europe or in Asia could have known how much they craved these marvelous ingredients during all those centuries when Jupiter and Saturn were lazily hooking up on the wheel of the Zodiac and the Admiral himself had yet to save a soul.

(The Turks, consolidated Islamic rule across the Middle East, harassing European trade along the old spice routes so that the Portuguese took to the sea around Africa and Columbus discovered America. So there!)

As soon as chiles were introduced into the bland diets of Europe, the people called them peppers anyway, just as Columbus had.

Besides, they were certainly as hot as black pepper, a lot hotter in fact so that their use in foods greatly increased the appeal of flat-tasting, wheat-based diets. Moreover, people didn't have to worry anymore about whether to go ahead and grind their five or six peppercorns for the scrambled eggs or just give them to the landlord to cover the rent.

Spain and Portugal: the seed bearers inspired by slaves

Spain got the chiles and peanuts into the Philippines, which became one of their territories in 1521, but it was Portugal who carried them everywhere else.

Because these traders wanted to cheaply satisfy the tastes and appetites of the slaves they dealt with and, because the enslaved people were extremely fond of peanuts, sweet potatoes and the hot chiles, these foods became virtual staples around coastal Africa and in the Orient.

Despite the closeness to North America, chiles remained unknown on these shores until the advent of the 17th Century slave trade. It was then that American plantations began growing the first chiles, peanuts and sweet potatoes transplanted from Africa because those foods had become integral to the diets of peoples all around that continent.

The genius who rediscovered the peanut

It is truly a remarkable circumstance that African people, brought here as slaves, inspired the plantation culture to grow these things before anyone else "discovered" them.

It is also fitting that George Washington Carver, a man born into slavery, became one of America's foremost agricultural inventors, developing over 350 uses for peanuts, sweet potatoes and pecans, which included printers inks and cosmetics, to say nothing of peanut butter.

Dr. Carver invented crop rotation in the South using peanuts as the means of both saving soil nutrients and improving agriculture. He turned down fabulous offers of money for his inventions, famously

DR. GEORGE WASHINGTON CARVER

saying "God gave them to me, how can I sell them to someone else?"

It is understandable that for 500 years people in the far east, Europe and North America assumed that Africa and Asia were where all chiles originated. The true origin probably got lost in generations of around-the-world trading combined with poor record keeping and the habit of assuming answers without evidence.

"Just take the money, Chris!"

Columbus made four voyages to the new world. He would have been better off had he stuck with two. He was rich, he was a hero and he had clout at the Court of Spain.

He ran into a nightmare in the islands on his third voyage. He was a terrible leader and an even worse administrator. He tried to rule everybody, not just the indians, with cruelty. The Spanish colonists whom he had helped settle there revolted, locked him up and sent him back to Spain in chains.

Subsequently these colonists continued the unbelievably cruel exploitation of the native peoples in their lust for gold. This episode remains a shameful testament to human greed and perhaps the most obsessive and disastrous case of gold fever ever recorded.

Columbus's fourth and last voyage, after redeeming himself to the king and queen, was a failed attempt to find the Indian Ocean. The principal reason that it was a failed attempt is that he attempted it in Central America! It nearly ended in mutiny when his weary, mosquito-bitten men started to feel that he may be nuts and that they might die just to boost his reputation.

Then disaster struck with a vengeance.

On July 1, 1502, he and the men on his ship survived the same hurricane which took 500 men and 29 out of the 30 gold-laden ships of the first Spanish treasure fleet to the bottom. The mind boggles at the level of folly and greed that must have blinded these people to their own humanity, say nothing of the humanity of the people they exploited.

Whatever else all that gold added up to, it certainly included a large measure of loss and misery which one has to note was just about the opposite of what they were looking for. We could do well to consider that hubris and folly are universal human traits that leave their mark on every "world age" including our own.

It was the lowly chile pepper and the peanut, among other indian gifts that gave the world true and lasting value.

The next time you order flaked red pepper for your pizza or have kung pao chicken or shrimp at a Chinese restaurant, you'll be enjoying some of the key ingredients that Columbus, the Spanish, the Portuguese, the African peoples and, most importantly, the American Indians contributed to the cuisine of the world – without ever knowing it. How strange it all seems in retrospect!

KUNG PAO CHICKEN OR SHRIMP

Serves 4 normal people or 2 excessively hungry ones.

The tools:

- Three or four small bowls
- Tablespoon
- Can opener
- Cook's knife
- Skillet (or wok if you prefer)

Note: *Many Chinese restaurants use dried red peppers, tossed in during or after cooking. However, I prefer cooking the fresh jalapenos in the food which results in a more robust, evenly distributed and flavorful taste as opposed to mere heat.*

Here's what you need from the store:

- 1 pound raw shrimp (peeled and deveined) or 1 pound chicken breast meat
- Garlic
- Dark (toasted) sesame oil
- 1 can sliced water chestnuts
- Soy sauce
- Dry roasted peanuts (salted/unsalted)
- 2 or 3 jalapeno chiles
- 1 small onion
- Celery
- 1 Red bell pepper
- Peanut oil
- Green onions
- Black pepper
- Corn starch (optional)
- 1 can LaChoy toasted rice noodles
- Long grain white rice

Here's how you put it together:

1. Put the raw shrimp or the raw chicken (cut into thin strips) into the bowl.

2. Add a clove or two of smashed garlic.

3. Add a half-spoonful of sesame oil, 4 big spoonfuls of the soy sauce and some peanut oil. Stir all this well. Cover while you . . .

4. . . . slice the onion (thinly) and place in a separate bowl.

5. Remove the seeds and white pithy matter from the jalapenos and slice the chiles into thin strips, adding them to the sliced onions.

6. Slice the already sliced water chestnuts and put them in there, too.

7. Chop 6 or 7 of the green onions into quarter-inch pieces and add them in.

8. Add a big handful of dry roasted peanuts to the vegetables.

9. Fry the vegetables in peanut oil or stir fry (high heat).

10. Add the marinated meat and stir until all is cooked (about 4 minutes).

11. *OPTIONAL:* Mix a small spoonful of cornstarch with a spoonful of cold water and stir in into the mix to thicken as it heats. Add a little water if necessary to get the right consistency. Serve with rice and small, CRISPY rice noodles.

Kung Pao, according to legend, originally was "Gong Bao," a well-known palace guardian in Szechuan who brought this dish back from an expedition. During the Cultural Revolution in the mid-sixties, Maoist zealots renamed Kung Pao to *"something fried as cubes,"* which may strike you as equally and comically cumbersome as Jefferson's *"potatoes fried in deep fat while raw, first having been cut into small slices."*

The rest of us went on calling it "Kung Pao."

Of birds, chiles and evolution

Birds eat even the hottest chiles apparently without noticing the heat. The seeds from the pods pass through their digestive systems, becoming a major means of propagating chiles everywhere. They have an almost limitless tolerance for *capsaicin*, the chemical that makes chiles *(capsicum fruits)* hot. Capsaicin is a compound of nitrogen which has an immediate effect on pain receptors in mammals but not in birds.

In fact, it is likely that capsicum plants have evolved this compound as a means of facilitating a wider dispersal than could be effected by mammals and that birds in their turn evolved capsaicin tolerance to insure themselves a food source "off limits" to mammals. Moreover, chiles contain very high amounts of vitamin A, which helps birds maintain healthy lungs.

The reason people frequently remove the seeds from the chiles they use is to reduce the heat level of the fruit; which is not actually in the seeds themselves but in the pithy material, or placenta, that holds the seeds inside the pod.

So keep in mind when you are "seeding" a jalapeno to cut out the white part that holds the seeds, otherwise your food might be a bit on the hot side.

Did you Know?

Since birds are not affected by the capsaicin in chiles and since mammals are, you can safely repel squirrels from your bird suet feeder by coating or blending the suet with cayenne pepper. This also would work in seed feeders except for the fact that the cayenne dust irritates the birds' eyes. BLACK PEPPER WILL NOT WORK!

THANKS, HERNANDO

Pigs got off the boat for the first time in North America near, what is now, Port Charlotte, Florida, on June 1, 1539, 39 years after Columbus made his last voyage. The ship was under the command of the famous conquistador/explorer, Hernando deSoto, who had come looking for (I needn't bother telling you) gold. The pigs were brought along as groceries.

DeSoto had 600 men with him, armed, some of them with shiny metal breast-plates and peaked metal helmets. Most of them were self-supplied just for a crack at getting some of that booty, the location of which deSoto was sure he was going to find by beating it out of the natives.

"Somebody tell those fellows to ride downwind"

These well-equipped conquistadores wound up travelling on foot and on horse-back all through the forests of, what now are, the states of Florida, Alabama, Georgia, the Carolinas, Tennessee, Kentucky and Illinois. *On foot and on horseback!* They looked for gold all the way to the shore of Lake Michigan then turned south and were credited with "discovering" the Mississippi River. They did all of this, remember, walking and riding horses through thick brush and across mountains without enough changes of socks and underwear, with no neosporin, no toothpaste, no shampoo and a no soap. It was 349 years before deodorant would be invented in Philadelphia.

DeSoto died in what would one day become Arkansas in May, 1542, and was tied to some rocks and buried in the river he discovered, perhaps to ensure that his aroma went with him. One assumes that most of the pigs had long become barbecue by then. Many of their descendants survived to share the same fate down through the years.

Great barbecue places across the American South use the Boston butt roast as the mainstay of their menus. They also serve ribs and even chicken. Many agree that the Boston butt is the only foundation, aside from baby back ribs, suitable for top-flight barbecue.

High on the hog in Jard sur Mer

Richard and Jenny Boxall, two dear British friends, had their second home in the little seaside town of Jard sur Mer, on France's west coast. They had invited my wife, Judy, and I there one summer for reasons of friendship and also to make pulled pork barbecue which they hoped to introduce to a few of their local friends. They knew that these people wouldn't recognize pulled pork barbecue if it walked up to them in full dress uniform.

They have pigs in Jard sur Mer but they don't have any barbecue. I don't think they have a lot of barbecue in England, either, because when I smoked a dry-rubbed Boston butt at my house in Pennsylvania one day, Richard asked how I intended to carve it, since the interior bones were aligned at odd angles.

"This is barbecue, Richard, you don't carve it. You grab ahold of it and pull it apart with your fingers."

"My God, you've got to be kidding," he said. "They would never do that in France."

The meat was almost sliding off the bone, so it was easy to separate it into beautiful, juicy chunks of steaming, hot pork and arrange them on a platter. It was as if I had worn flip-flops to meet The Queen.

I stabbed a small piece with a knife and held it out to him. "Well, we ain't in France," I said. He took that morsel and savored it and in an instant became a born-again fan of pulled pork barbecue.

Richard asked if I would do the pulled pork for his French friends who would think it unique. There is no cut of pork known as Boston butt anywhere in France (the reason for which appears below) so we bought a reasonable substitute from some other part of the pig and it worked.

But it's not a butt

This cut is actually the shoulder of the hog; a roast which is cut *"high on the hog,"* thus to obtain the premium portion. It is not a true butt roast at all.

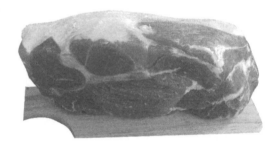

It's always best to get a shoulder roast that has the bone in it rather than removed. Carving at the table is not a problem because the slow cooking for 8-10 hours will make the meat come easily off the bone in big, juicy "pulled" chunks.

What's Boston got to do with it?

These large cuts of meat were kept in storage in wooden barrels in New England around the time of the American Revolution. The barrels were called "butts," the old English version of the French "botte," or pipe. A butt held 108 imperial gallons or several dozen shoulder roasts. In the Boston area this cut of pork shoulder became known as the Boston butt. The name stuck and has continued into the modern era – everywhere except in Boston.

The full-sized, bone-in Boston butt will weigh eight to 12 pounds but you can get smaller ones or have the butcher cut the big ones in half. You can get either a blade shoulder roast or an arm shoulder. I prefer the blade.

Here's how to do one on the domed Weber grill:

BARBECUED BOSTON BUTT

1. Dry rub the meat with Lawry's Seasoned Salt, lots of black pepper and a small amount of dried, Greek oregano.

2. Don't trim off any of the fat.

3. Place the roast on a charcoal grill with the hot coals on one side and the meat on the other.

   When the coals are ready, put the meat on the grill on the opposite side from where the hot coals are and check the clock.

4. Vent both the bottom and top vents the same width as a pencil thickness.

5. Leave the grill covered for 4-5 hours then add a few more pieces of charcoal. You can add small bits of wood to the fire, too, just be sure that you use a wood that imparts good flavor. The best wood for barbecue is hickory and you want it to smoke, not to burn vigorously. Figure on roasting this cut for one hour per pound and pay no attention to recipes that tell you 30 minutes a pound will do. Turn the roast occasionally.

6. Remove when the meat starts to slide off the bone, regardless of how much or how little time it takes. During the cooking, you may continue to add fresh wood sparingly. You want to avoid starting a big blaze.

A friend and neighbor of mine did a Boston butt on his gas grill for July 4th and took it off after 40 minutes per pound. It looked great from the outside but the meat clung to the bone. When cut, this roast was obviously not ready. I can assure you that nothing can be done to rescue a Boston butt after this has happened. Allow more time than you think it will take.

You should never use a gas grill to do one of these. You will be disappointed every time. Stick to charcoal and raw wood.

I prefer genuine wood charcoal over briquettes but briquettes work fine. If you do supplement with pieces of wood, your results will be better. A lot of people like to use mesquite but it has too much of its own flavor for pork roasts and works better when you are grilling steaks. A 10-pound Boston butt will weigh about eight pounds when it's ready and seven hours of mesquite smoking overpowers the flavors of the meat.

Boston also gave its name to baked beans, despite the fact that they originated thousands of miles to the south. Beans are great with barbecue.

BARBECUE PORK SHOULDER – WET OR DRY?

A quality Boston butt roast will be laced through with enough fat to obviate the need for barbecue sauce, which is why you may prefer a dry rub.

However, if you must lather the meat up with sauce while it cooks, avoid the over-sweet pomades they call barbecue sauce at the supermarket. They are made with thick tomato reductions, chili powder, smoke flavoring, mustard, sugar and preservative chemicals and they tend to become charred, candified tar on the surface of your roast.

There is a "penetrating" sauce containing neither tomatoes nor sugar used for mopping chicken on an uncovered grill. It works on a pork shoulder, too, but should be used mainly to moisten the surface close to the time the meat has fully cooked.

"PENETRATING" BARBECUE SAUCE

Bring the sauce to a gentle boil and then it's ready to go.

The tools:
- Barbeque mop
- Large pot

Here's what you need from the store:
- 1 pound unsalted butter
- 1 pint apple cider vinegar
- Worcestershire sauce
- Garlic salt
- Salt
- Paprika

Here's how you put it together:

1. Pour the pint of vinegar into a pot and turn the heat to medium.
2. Add all four sticks of unsalted butter.
3. Add 8 Tablespoons Worcestershire.
4. Add 1 Tablespoon garlic salt.
5. Add 1 Tablespoon regular salt.
6. Add 1 Tablespoon paprika.
7. Heat just to boiling, stir and remove to a spot near your grill. Mop on the surface of the meat every 20 minutes or so.

A conjecture concerning pork taboos

The origin of the taboo against eating pigs, proscribed both by the Torah and the Koran, may have been inspired by the fact that pig meat, particularly in hot, arid lands, can harbor a number of parasites which cause disease.

My uneducated guess is that the pig taboo, like others, started from efforts by the tribal leadership of those societies to maintain the health of the gene pool by inter-generational avoidance of unclean meat.

This injunction probably would not have worked if people suspected it came from laws made by mere humans so the Almighty was assigned authorship of it in order to make it stick. You might get away with messing with your shaman every now and then but not He Who Regulates The Universe.

But getting back to barbecue.

The word itself comes from the Caribbean Arawakan indian "barbacoa," the name given in their Taino tongue to a laced mat of green wood on which meat was slowly roasted over hot coals.

You should keep in mind that smoker-cooked meats are not the same as those done on over an open pit and that too much smoke infusion can adversely affect the flavor of the meat. Open-pit cooking or freely-vented cooking provides just the amount needed to impart the desired flavors of classic barbecue. American barbecue is a time-honored thing which uses time as one of its key components. The church picnic established its lasting place in American cooking. You put the meat on at dawn and by the time the preacher wound down and the choir stopped singing it was ready.

OTHER EXCUSES: BEAN BURRITOS AND HUEVOS RANCHEROS

Barbecue is just one of countless good excuses to use hot chiles or compounds derived from them. I have done Boston butts that were delicious by simply mop-ping them a couple of times with pure, unalloyed Tabasco sauce and have enjoyed catfish fillets marinated in Tabasco before frying. Believe it or not, this results in a taste which is not suicidally hot.

Once you experience the tastes of chiles and their almost magical warmth there usually is no turning back.

Also, there is a difference in the tastes of foods that are seasoned with dried chile flakes after cooking and foods in which freshly chopped chiles are cooked with the food. The flavors and heat of the fresh chiles permeate as cooking takes place result-ing in a much more appealing warmth. It is the difference you might expect from heat "applied" to food and warmth "included" with food. It comes from within.

In 1911, Wilbur Scoville, an author and pharmacologist at the Parke Davis phar-maceutical company, invented a scale to measure the perceived heat intensity of various chiles. He knew that chemicals called "capsaicinoids" were what caused the heat sensation.

Scoville's test is known simply enough as the *"Scoville Organaloptic Test"* and it determines the amount of sugar water needed to dilute the capsaicinoids in any given chile pepper before the heat becomes no longer noticeable.

You might imagine that the Scoville model could be copied and used in other applications. For example, you may be able to develop an accurate measure for how much bourbon is needed to neutralize the effect of listening to a congressman.

How hot is it?

Pure capsaicin	16,000,000
Habanero	100,000 - 350,000
Scotch Bonnet	100,000 - 325,000
Birds Eye	100,000 - 225,000
Cayenne Chile	100,000 - 125,000
Thai Chile	50,000 - 100,000
Tabasco Chile	30,000 - 50,000
TABASCO	2,500 - 5,000
Jalapeno	2,500 - 5,000
Ancho Chile	1,000 - 2,000
Poblano	1,000 - 2,000
Pimento	100 - 500
Bell Pepper	0

You could never dream this up

The economic importance of chiles and peanuts is in the billions of dollars worldwide and the cultural impact is incalculable. The trade in just these two commodities supports millions of people in hundreds of thousands of endeavors in practically every country in the world. Certainly, neither the King and Queen of Spain nor Columbus could have foreseen this. They were driven by a lust for gold and limited by their own expectations.

This has to rank as one of the biggest and most monumentally profitable unintended consequences of all time. And please note, it was not the result of people sitting in a legislative body in Europe, thinking they were smart enough to change the world. No. The potato changed the world. The self-impressed heads of state never saw it coming. They still see nothing coming!

So, where is the gold of El Dorado today?

Much of it went to the bottom of the sea, much of it went to Spain's rulers to finance wars which would deplete the treasury. Some of it sits in museums. But none of it can ever equal a fraction of the value of the indigenous foods of the Americas which the Spaniards brought back from the indians.

The lowly potato, with thousands of varieties still being cultivated today in Peru and the Andes where it originated, may appropriately be labeled the real gold of the Incas with the native crown jewels being such additions to the kitchens of the world as corn, squash, avocados, tomatoes, beans, chocolate, and all the rest.

The gnarly little lump that saved Europe

The first potato discovered by the Spaniards in the New World was the sweet potato. The Incas of Peru referred to it as "batata" which, obviously is the verbal parent of "potato."

There are at least 4,000 varieties of potatoes known to exist. They have been cultivated by humans for 6,000 years and have become the fourth biggest source of plant food for humans in the world, after rice, wheat and corn.

In 1845, the Great Potato Famine struck the counties of western Ireland, partly because the potato crop was limited to a single variety. The American Indians had given the world the potato. They made another gift in 1847.

Halfway into the famine, a group of Choctaw Indians in Oklahoma collected $710 and sent it to help the people of Ireland who were starving. In 1997, Irish President Mary Robinson publicly commemorated this amazing gift on its 150th anniversary.

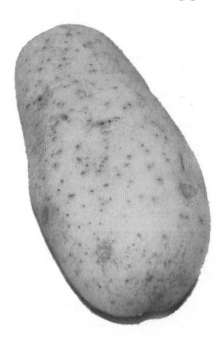

CHEESEY HASH BROWNS

Serves 8 as a side dish

The tools:
- Cook's knife
- Cutting board
- Big skillet (real big!)
- Coffee mug/measuring cup
- Big bowl
- Medium bowl
- 9" x 13" x 2" baking dish
- Vegetable grater
- Gallon-Ziplock bags

Here's what you need from the store:
- 6 medium-sized red potatoes
- Bacon
- Onion
- Jalapeno chiles
- Butter
- Flour
- Half & half
- Chicken base paste
- Grated yellow cheddar cheese
- Corn flakes (optional, see directions)

Here's how you put it together:

1. Make the hash browns:

   a. Fry 4 strips of bacon in the skillet then remove, drain & crumble.

   b. Thin-slice the onions and let them slowly caramelize in the skillet on medium heat (about 18 minutes).

   c. Add 1 chopped jalapeno, the grated potatoes and turn the heat to medium-high and fry until the potatoes are golden brown.

2. Put all this into the baking dish. Sprinkle the crumbled bacon over it.

3. Melt a third stick of butter in the skillet.

4. Add a spoonful of flour and blend.

5. Add a spoonful of chicken base and blend (replaces the salt).

6. Slowly stir in a pint of half & half and allow to thicken.

7. Add 1 mug of grated, mild, yellow cheddar cheese and blend.

8. Pour the cheese sauce over the hash browns & bake at 350 degrees for 45 minutes.

9. *OPTIONAL:* In the small bowl, mix 1 cup corn flakes (which have been smashed in a ziplock bag) with some melted butter. Then spread this across the top of the hash browns and cheese sauce before baking.

LUNCH WITH MONTEZUMA

MONTEZUMA

In 1492, Bernal Diaz Castillo was born in Medina del Campo, Spain, to prominent parents of modest means. That is about all anybody knows of him until he joined a company that set sail for the world Columbus discovered in the year of Bernal's birth. Adventuring in the Caribbean under several explorers, he wound up with Hernando Cortez (also spelled Cortes) who subsequently led the expedition that conquered Mexico.

His book; *The Discovery and Conquest of Mexico* is fascinating because it is an eyewitness account of the battles which caused the downfall of the Aztec empire and its king, Montezuma. A lot of the history you read is researched but this is the straight scoop from a guy who was there and went through it all. It is a fascinating account of bravery, treachery, warfare, death and the horrors of human sacrifice. In one excerpt he writes:

"There were piles of human skulls so regularly arranged that one could count them, and I estimated them at more than a hundred thousand. I repeat again that there were more than one hundred thousand of them."

He writes in detail how the Aztec priests hacked up the sacrificial, human victims and sold the various cuts in a meat market *"the same as our butcher shops do at home."*

Bernal describes the elaborate way in which Montezuma was served, with none of the high-ranking members of the court allowed to look directly at him. He received wild game, fruits and a bitter chocolate drink ("xocoatl") in cups of solid gold. The servants were forced to look away as they placed the dishes before him.

None of the Spaniards had ever witnessed human sacrifice and when Cortez expressed his displeasure to Montezuma and asked that he be allowed to build a Christian shrine he received a severe reprimand and was told to pray before the Aztec gods.

The inevitable clash of Aztec and European civilizations resulted in the complete devastation of the Mexican capitol and the end of its culture of death.

But, possibly with the exception of butchered humans, the food was good!

One of the many dishes that would have been served to Montezuma is a posole or a stew made with meat, chiles and hominy. The meat used in it today is pork shoulder, but in the time of Montezuma it would have been either dog, turkey or duck, the only animals, aside from hapless human sacrificial victims, exclusively raised or slaughtered for meat in the Aztec culture. Montezuma and his courtiers also would have eaten tortillas and tacos, probably without inquiring where the meat came from.

"North of the border"

We used to sell the pies from our pie company to restaurant distributors along the Atlantic Seaboard. Once, while visiting Mexican restaurants in Atlanta with my salesman, Denny Smith, an inspiration from all those kitchens began to manifest itself into a fully developed craving.

By late afternoon, that craving had become specifically southwest-oriented so the two of us determined that it should inspire supper. Since I was staying at Denny's house, I figured it might take the place of rent, which, in this case, would have been drinks, a bottle of wine and a steak dinner at a three-star restaurant with me picking up the tab.

I cautiously refer to this plan as "Southwest style" because even though I have eaten my way across parts of Mexico and Texas, I am definitely not the go-to guy for Tex-Mex. A *real* go-to guy for Tex-Mex would just go ahead and go to the three-star restaurant.

This plan involves a cornbread batter poured over the other ingredients. As the whole thing bakes, the batter sets up, forming a "roof" that seals in all the flavors and provides a delicious, bready accompaniment to the chicken and vegetables.

SOUTHWEST STYLE CHICKEN

SOUTHWEST STYLE CHICKEN

Serves 4

The tools:
- Cutting board
- Cook's knife
- Bowl
- Large spoon
- 3-quart baking dish
- Whisk

Here's what you need from the store:
- 1 large, skinned and boned chicken breast and a couple of boned thighs
- Lawry's Seasoned Salt
- Bacon
- 1 large onion
- Celery
- Dried oregano
- 2 or 3 jalapeno chiles
- 3 green onions
- Mexican grated cheese blend or similar mild grated cheese
- Chili powder
- Salt & black pepper to taste
- Peanut oil or olive oil
- 1 small can creamed corn
- 1 package Bob's Red Barn corn meal
- Baking powder
- Eggs
- Half & half or buttermilk (but not both)

Here's how you put it together:

1. Cut the chicken meat into pieces, sprinkle with seasoned salt and fry in some oil until just turning golden. Put this aside in a bowl.

2. Chop 4 slices bacon into bits and fry in the skillet until crispy.

3. Chop 3 seeded jalapenos, 3 green onions, some parsley, celery and 1 onion and add this to the bacon in the skillet.

5. When soft, distribute the vegetables across the bottom of the baking dish.

6. Sprinkle this evenly with some chili powder and a little oregano.

7. Distribute the cooked chicken over this.

8. Distribute half the cheese across the top.

9. Repeat the layers.

10. For the topping (you want this to be runny), blend the cornbread ingredients and pour evenly over the whole thing:

    *One cup **Bob's Red Barn** stone ground yellow corn meal or similar, 1 small can creamed corn, two teaspoons baking powder, two large eggs, half teaspoon salt, quarter cup peanut oil, 3/4 pint half & half. Blend this well with a whisk, pour on top.*

11. Bake at 350 degrees for 30 minutes.

PEPPERY CORN PUDDING

Serves 6 as a side dish

Anybody who loves the aromas and flavors of corn will appreciate this delicious corn pudding. You'll need a blender, but if you don't have one, borrow it from a friend because you'll be glad you made this.

The tools:
- Blender
- Cutting board
- Cook's knife
- Coffee mug
- Tablespoon
- Large bowl

Here's what you need from the store:
- 1 big package frozen white corn (or fresh corn cut off the cob)
- Eggs
- 1 quart half & half
- 1 pound grated mild yellow cheddar cheese
- Unsalted butter
- Regular flour
- Chicken base paste
- Red pepper flakes
- Black pepper

Here's how you put it together:

1. Preheat oven to 350 degrees.
2. Put half a package of the corn into the blender.
3. Add 6 eggs.
4. Add 2 cups of the half & half.
5. Blend until smooth then pour into a large bowl.
6. Repeat with the remaining corn and half & half and add this to the large bowl.
7. Melt a stick of butter in a skillet on medium heat.
8. Whisk in 2 tablespoons flour and blend well.
9. Add a spoonful of chicken base paste.
10. Add some red pepper flakes and some black pepper. Blend well.
11. Add this to the large bowl.
12. Briskly whisk all this together until smooth.
13. Add half the cheese, blend it in, then pour into a baking dish.
14. Sprinkle remaining cheese on top.
15. Bake at 350 degrees for 30-40 minutes or until the pudding is "set" (The top springs back when lightly tapped).

POSOLE

Serves 8

This is a hearty stew or heavy soup and quite likely the original version of what today we call "chili." It is traditionally made with hominy. You could use canned hominy but I don't recommend it; getting fresh hominy is not only difficult but cooking it takes a long time. I use only whole kernel white corn, which gives the stew a distinct richness and sweetness, especially if you cut it fresh, right off the cob. Even without the hominy, Montezuma would still have recognized this.

The tools:

- Cook's knife
- Cutting board
- Skillet for browning
- Large pot
- Small pot
- Blender

Here's what you need from the store:

- 2 pounds boneless pork shoulder
- 6-8 dried Anchos chile peppers
- Garlic
- Jalapeno chiles
- Chicken base paste
- Olive oil
- Dried oregano
- 2 cans white hominy or an equivalent amount of frozen white corn kernels
- Gravy Master

Here's how you put it together:

1. Cut the pork into small pieces and brown it in a liberal amount of oil.

2. Cut the dried chiles with scissors, removing the seeds, and put them in the small pot with just enough water to cover and simmer until tender. (About 10 minutes).

3. Add just enough water to cover the already browned meat in the skillet and simmer it on medium heat.

4. When the chiles are tender, put them in a blender with a small amount of the cooking water.

5. Add 2 or 3 seeded jalapenos, 2 or 3 cloves of garlic and some dried oregano and blend until smooth.

6. Add this mix to the simmering meat with a spoonful of the Gravy Master.

7. Add a spoonful of the chicken base and black pepper to taste.

8. Add the raw corn kernels (or, if you like, the hominy).

9. Simmer on low until the meat is tender and the broth is thick (2 hours) adding small amounts of water as needed.

10. Serve with chopped onion, green onion, grated cheddar cheese, shredded lettuce* hot, buttered cornbread or cornbread muffins. (*I ditch the lettuce).

CORNBREAD MUFFINS

The tools:
- Muffin tin
- Muffin cup papers
- Large bowl
- Whisk
- Tablespoon
- Teaspoon
- Mug or cup

Here's what you need from the store:
- Stone ground yellow cornmeal*
  (Bob's Red Barn packs a good one)
- Eggs
- King Arthur whole wheat flour
- Unsalted butter
- Baking powder
- Baking soda
- Salt
- Buttermilk

Any quality cornmeal will work but you can order freshly stone ground online: www. oakviewfarms.com

Here's how you put it together:

1. Mix 1-3/4 cups of cornmeal with 3/4 cup of flour in a 2-quart bowl.

2. Blend in 4 teaspoons of baking powder, 1/2 teaspoon baking soda and 3/4 teaspoon of salt.

3. In a small bowl, whisk together 1 stick of melted butter, 2 regular sized eggs and 1-3/4 cups buttermilk.

4. Pour the liquid directly onto the dry mix and whisk until blended.

5. Spoon into muffin cups and bake at 425 degrees for 22 minutes.

The opposite "stars" who are one and the same

QUETZALCOATL
Codex Borgia

The twin Aztec deities, Quetzalcoatl and Tezcatlipoca represented, among other things, light and dark. Quetzalcoatl was the planet Venus as a bright morning star, rising before the sun and Tezcatlipoca by the same planet as a "dark" evening star, setting after the sun. Montezuma, according to reports sent back to Spain, is said to have believed that Cortez was the manifestation of Quetzalcoatl, who had come to them out of the east in human form. Cortez believed that Montezuma saw him that way and was so impressed by the king's gullibility that he wrote to his Spanish king glowing accounts of it.

Montezuma may have been employing the Aztec version of diplomatic flim-flam which involved the heavy use of flattery and hospitality to give an opponent a false sense of security.

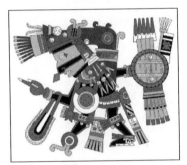

TEZCATLIPOCA
Codex Borgia

Still, it is worth noting that the Aztec religion had, by that time, long associated Quetzalcoatl *with the year known to Europeans as 1519 A.D.; the same year that Cortez, having sailed from the east, landed with his men in Mexico!* This was an incredible (and you could say monumentally unfortunate) coincidence.

If you plot on the wheel of the Zodiac the two opposite cyclical occurrences of Venus rising just ahead of the sun and then setting just after the sun, you will form two identical series of lines across the wheel of the Zodiac that make a five-pointed star every eight years for each sequence. Aztec and Mayan temples were aligned precisely to observe these 8-year cycles as well as to track the movements of the sun and the other planets. They shared with the Maya an astounding science of celestial documentation which led to the development of calendars far more accurate than any developed in Europe. This same planet was followed by ancient astronomers all around the world for thousands of years and was known in mythology outside of the Americas mostly as a female deity: Innana, Astarte, Ishtar and Aphrodite.

No less than the Pythagoreans of ancient Greece and the mythographer-astronomers of the west, the Aztecs had their own understanding of the end of one world age and the beginning of the next and they used the same planets in their predictions.

Regardless of the imaginings of doomsayers, Jupiter and Saturn will go on battling it out in their regular conjunctions and Venus will still be both the "evening star" and the "morning star" to those who care to look to the horizon as the Aztecs and the Maya did from their dark temples of a thousand years ago.

Signs and wonders!

Such planetary behavior was almost certainly seen by ancient peoples as being done by "intelligence" not mere points of light or lifeless planets. Their cycles indicated that they must surely have "known" what they were doing. They kept this up while changing positions in the sky and, sooner or later repeatedly wound up in the same place on the wheel of time. The stars of the sky were moving in lockstep as if on a slowly revolving dome.

Moreover, the planets shifted around with what must have seemed an astounding regularity over very long periods of time. What were they doing out there? What were they telling us?

Any guess would have been wrong but most early peoples were convinced that they knew and sacrificed millions of fellow humans over the millennia to keep these cycles going.

Staying up with planetary movements was not a waste of time, however. It is thought by some to have given our remote ancestors the first awareness of the importance of number.

This knowledge, accumulated and refined over thousands of generations and recorded on cave walls, antlers and rocks, became the earliest foundation of mathematics and science long before the "dawn" of what we call history. On a more mundane level, these "patterns" reinforced a mystical belief in the myth of multiple gods and the eternal return. Today, they are used to prove much popular nonsense regarding "influences" among we smog-infested, light-polluted readers of tabloid newspapers and end-of-the-world forecasters; watching our televisions as Montezuma must have watched the night sky.

Did You Know?

Each appearance of the planet Venus as a morning star happens 72 degrees farther along the Zodiacal circle. The cycle repeats every 8 years. It does the same thing as an evening star. Thus 8 years is the principal number related to the planet. For Saturn, the period is 59 years, Jupiter 71, Mars 79 and Mercury 46 years.

Venus is the heavenly timekeeper and guarantor of reliability.

From: Giorgio de Santillana's book; "Reflections on Men and Ideas" (M.I.T.)

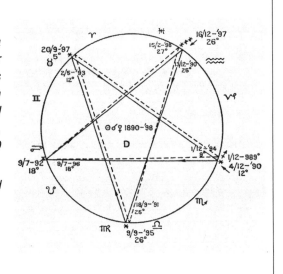

38

Notes _____

_____

_____

_____

_____

_____

_____

_____

_____

_____

_____

_____

_____

_____

_____

_____

_____

_____

_____

_____

_____

_____

_____

_____

_____

"Liberty Leading the People" Eugene Delacroix, 1830

Some French Influences

JEAN-BAPTISTE DONATIEN DE VIMEUR,
COMTE DE ROCHAMBEAU

The surrender of the British at Yorktown, Virginia, which effectively ended the Revolutionary War, was made possible by the intervention of French forces in the late summer of 1781. It was, as the Brits might say, a close run thing. General George Washington, already the literal and figurative father of his country, was a hard man to persuade when his mind was made up and by the early summer of 1781, his mind was focused on fighting the British in New York, where he and his army were set to do battle.

However, as fortune would have it, Washington learned from his French Aide de Camp, Lt. Col. (Marquis) de Lafayette, that French Admiral de Grasse was heading for the Chesapeake and correctly assumed that this would give the Americans a better shot at victory. If de Grasse could block the British Navy from reinforcing their southern command at Yorktown then the British army could be trapped. And so they were.

The French General, Rochambeau, with his 6,000 French soldiers, combined with a contingent of American troops under his command, added the critical mass needed by Washington. Together, they stealthily marched their armies out of New York without the British finding out until it was too late.

SURRENDER AT YORKTOWN ON OCTOBER 19, 1781, COMMISSIONED BY ARTIST JOHN TRUMBULL IN 1817. CORNWALLIS HIMSELF IS NOT DEPICTED BECAUSE HE WAS NOT PRESENT AT THE SURRENDER. SOURCE: WIKIMEDIA, COURTESY OF THE ARCHITECT OF THE CAPITOL, WASHINGTON, D.C.

The man of the hour

Not only was Rochambeau an important ally in the war but he commanded American soldiers under Washington and thus served as a defacto American officer against the British. It was Rochambeau who drew from his own personal account enough cash (then the sum of $20,000) to allow Washington to pay his troops' salaries when Congress was unable to raise the money in time.

A bronze statue of Rochambeau stands today across Pennsylvania Avenue from the White House. Appropriately it is in Lafayette Park, named after his compatriot, Marquis de Lafayette, who appears in a line of three American officers, who stand on the far right of the painting. Included in that line are Lt. Col. Alexander Hamilton and Lt. Col John Laurens.

Col. Laurens, age 26, from South Carolina, drew up the terms of the surrender. He was the son of Henry Laurens, prior president of the Continental Congress and, on that day, a prisoner being held in the Tower of London. He had been captured by a British frigate on the high seas while on a mission to Holland to raise money for the war.

One of the terms of the surrender was that Cornwallis, rather than being taken prisoner, was to be paroled and exchanged for Henry Laurens and this is what happened. Laurens went from London directly to Paris, where he joined the American diplomatic contingent in drawing up the Treaty of Paris, by which England formally recognized the sovereignty of the United States.

The irony could not have been lost on either of the Laurenses that one of the titles of Lord Cornwallis at that time was "Constable of the Tower of London."

Rochambeau insisted that the British under Cornwallis surrender to the Americans not to the French, as some maintain Cornwallis probably had requested. Cornwallis, ever a bitter and nasty opponent, refused to attend the surrender claiming he was too ill to go out, although artists of some of the paintings used "artistic license" to depict him there.

He went on to greater fame and glory as Governor-General of India. Ironically, Cornwallis reputedly had supported the American cause before the outbreak of hostilities.

Almost as good as having a statue raised in your honor is having a special dish named after you on the menu of a long-famous and highly respected restaurant.

Generations after Cornwallis arrogantly stayed in his tent at Yorktown, a chef at the famous Antoine's Restaurant in New Orleans' French Quarter invented a dish and named it after the French general who so greatly aided America's victory.

GENERAL ROCHAMBEAU
PENNSYLVANIA AVENUE, WASHINGTON D.C.

CHICKEN ROCHAMBEAU

Serves 4

There are five major components involved in making this recipe: mushroom sauce, butter-sauteed chicken breast, fried ham slices, bearnaise sauce and toasted french bread.

The tools:

- Double boiler
- Cutting board
- Cook's knife
- Skillet
- Coffee mug/cup
- Saucepan or cook pot
- Garlic press
- Whisk
- Tablespoon
- Teaspoon
- 2 small bowls

You can make this by yourself in about an hour. However, if you can get people to help with various elements, you and they can get this to the table in half that time and have twice as much fun.

Here's what you need from the store:

- 4 boned, thin sliced chicken breasts
- Ham, sliced 1/8 inch
- Mushrooms
- 1 bunch green onions
- Fresh parsley
- Flour
- Olive oil
- Butter/salt/pepper
- Tarragon (dry)
- White wine
- Eggs
- Tarragon vinegar
- Lemon
- Black pepper
- Gravy Master
- Chicken base paste
- French bread

1. Make the Mushroom Sauce:

1. Chop two handfuls of mushrooms into small bits.
2. Fry the chopped mushrooms in olive oil on high for 3 minutes then turn heat to medium-low.
3. Sprinkle a small spoonful of flour on the mushrooms and mix completely.
4. Add a handful of very finely chopped green onion tops.
5. Add a spoonful of the Gravy Master.
6. Add water and stir until sauce is thick and syrupy (like a stew).
7. Season with a spoonful of chicken base paste & black pepper.
8. Set this aside.

2. Cook the Chicken and Ham:

1. Season the chicken with salt & pepper and shake in a ziplock bag with some flour to lightly coat.
2. Fry gently in butter until golden. Set aside in a warm place and cover.
3. In the same skillet, gently fry the ham slices in butter; one minute each side. Place with the chicken breasts and re-cover to keep warm.

3. Make the Bearnaise Sauce:

1. Place a double boiler on the stove top with about a half-inch of water in the bottom. (You can jury rig this with a 2-quart pot and a metal bowl with a rounded bottom that fits into it. You will need a towel to hold the bowl with).
2. Melt one stick of butter in a separate container.
3. Before turning the heat on, put the following into the bowl or the top section of the double boiler:

   a. 2 tablespoons tarragon vinegar and a sprinkle of salt

   b. 2 tablespoons fresh squeezed lemon juice

   c. 8 jumbo egg yolks (you can save the whites in the refrigerator and use them later in scrambled eggs)

4. Turn the heat to medium, whisk constantly at a slow, steady pace so that the yolks can coagulate smoothly. If you see bits of yolk starting to form, quickly remove the pot from the heat and continue whisking briskly. Return to the heat. The idea is to cook the mixture without solidifying it.
5. Keep whisking. When the yolk mixture gets thick, remove the pot from the heat.
6. Add a half-spoonful of dry tarragon to the egg mixture and while still hot and obviously thicker, slowly drizzle the melted butter into it, whisking constantly.
7. That's it. (You can keep this warm by covering the bowl and leaving it on the stove with the heat turned off).

4. Toast the French Bread.

5. Assemble on Serving Plates as follows:

1. Toasted bread
2. Ham slice
3. Mushroom sauce
4. Chicken breast
5. Bearnaise sauce

This looks hard to do but, trust me, it isn't. It helps to lay things out, get all the stuff chopped and positioned ahead of time and then take a minute to think through the whole process, step by step. You will be impressed with yourself and your guests will think they have had dinner at Antoine's, even if they had a hand in making it.

Make sure your meats are tender

You ought to be able to eat this with a fork but even though you don't it still should be tender. If you can't get tender ham, get the deli to slice some paper-thin and use several slices of that (heated) instead of a thick single slice.

Sometimes even thin-sliced chicken breasts can be tough but the solution is easy; gently pound the slices with the smooth side of a mallet so that they flatten slightly. The flattening separates some of the tissues in the meat, making it tender. If you don't have a mallet you can use an unopened bottle of wine by laying an olive-oiled sheet of plastic food wrap over the meat. Easy does it. You'll get results after a few dozen moderate blows on the cutting board.

BY WAY OF LOBSTER

French cuisine has been familiar to taste buds in New Orleans since the city's founding by Jean Baptiste Le Moyne in 1718. Much of it has been adapted to use local ingredients and has changed over the years but you can still enjoy French culinary styles in New Orleans. It's a good-eatin' town, whether genuinely French or not. French and Spanish and French Creole are definitely predominant.

The French, by the way, have a saying that "the way to a man's heart is by way of his sex; the way to a woman's sex is by way of her heart."

People make millions publishing whole books that say less than that.

Here's an idea for another one: "the way to a woman's heart is by way of lobster." Why do women love lobster? What makes lobster the number one menu choice for most females? If you can't figure it out just trust the maxim: women love lobster!

In the Azores, get the "lagosta"

Sao Miguel is one of the volcanic islands of the Azores, a Portuguese archipelago lying 950 miles out in the Atlantic, west of the mainland. They eat a lot of lobster in the Azores. It was there, during a memorable lobster lunch, that I learned about vinho verde (named for its pale, green tint), a delightful Portuguese wine which nicely accompanies delicate foods.

Four French journalists and I had packed ourselves into a rented Renault subcompact to drive from the tiny port of Ponta Delgada, Sao Miguel, all the way to the volcanic top of the island to do some hiking.

Switzerland in the Atlantic?

Occasionally we would be immersed in heavy fog as a cloud moved across the mountain. You could hear cow bells out there somewhere on the slope. We stopped at a tiny stone barn, which appeared very old. Inside, a man and his son were making cheese in a one-piece, carved stone vat the size of a bathtub. The older man tried to indicate the process through sign language but was too busy to entertain us beyond that.

We left the pair to their labors and squeezed back into the car and drove away, past an audience of silent cows.

Then, just as suddenly, the sun reappeared in a deep blue sky and we could see the top of the volcano.

From the summit, nearly 1,800 feet above the ocean, you could see, nestled inside the lake-filled crater, a village, referred to on maps and promotional pieces as "Sete Cidades," or "seven cities"; long a part of Atlantean myth in that region. We were able to see but one from our vantage point. And, although quaint, it was more a fragment of mythology left over from the Middle Ages than a city.

At around noon we drove into the seacoast village of Mosteiros, tired from hiking and hungry. We saw nothing but tidy homes along a narrow street through town.

As we were about to leave Mosteiros, probably forever, Claude Benoit, who was driving, pulled to a stop in front of one of the homes. In a window, rimmed with lace curtains and barely visible was a small, handmade sign with the word "restaurante" printed in pencil. It was enough. Our hungry eyes had found it.

The family seated us at a large table in the unadorned and empty front room and asked what we wanted. There was no menu. "What do you suggest?" we asked in broken Portuguese.

"Lagosta," the man replied.

And with that he and his wife disappeared, leaving a waiter of about 14 years, apparently their son, to bring us two bottles of cold vinho verde, some glasses and a basket of freshly-baked bread.

This inexpensive Portuguese specialty wine is a sweetly acidic match for seafood and goes especially well with lobster. It's not elegant or refined because it is drunk while still young but it makes a very good, refreshing drink. You have to be careful buying it in the United States, however, since the quality is only at its peak for about a year after being bottled.

It was sweet to sit with friends in that little place. But there were church bells tolling in the distance. There also was the sound of a drum being beaten slowly and rhythmically and approaching up the street.

Our host informed us that a young man from the village had been killed serving in the Portuguese army in Angola and that his body had been returned for burial.

Two brothers were among the pall bearers, neither showing emotion. Behind the casket wailed his mother and some aunts.

They were draped in black with veils of white lace. The young man's father accompanied them in front, his face stained with tears. The owner solemnly provided this narrative.

We all stood from the table in respectful silence and when the procession had passed and we were once again seated at the table, Claude raised his glass.

"To life," he said. We drank to the dead soldier.

Moments later, the host and his wife reappeared with a silver platter, mounded with what appeared to be eight large, whole lobsters, bright red and steaming.

Why anybody would want to enjoy lobster prepared in any other way than as-is seems a mystery. However, there is lobster stew, stuffed lobster, lobster bisque, lobster salad, lobster fondue, fried lobster, lobster primavera and two well-known favorites, lobster newberg and lobster thermidor.

They all are good.

"THE HOT ONE"

At a place for lunch in Boston a few years back, the waiter talked us into a creamed lobster on rice, which was listed on the menu as "The Hot One" and advertised as heavily seasoned with Tabasco.

The taste of almost any seafood is so greatly enhanced by the addition of Tabasco that it is hard to resist.

The caveat is that you really do need to use authentic Tabasco and not one of the many Tabasco wannabes. Only Tabasco has its own peculiarly unique flavor; the result of a proprietary process that requires aging in oak whiskey barrels for up to three years.

Tabasco is so important to my seafood dishes that I would classify it almost as a key ingredient.

Tabasco is great in crab louis, shrimp or crawfish etouffee, crabmeat crepes, oysters on the halfshell, fried scallops, any sort of seafood bisque, seafood pasta, king crab legs, blue crab claws, oyster cocktail, any cream-based dish such as lobster thermidor, crab or lobster casserole and also in oyster or shrimp cocktail or sprinkled on fried fish or crab cakes.

SOME FIXIN'S FOR THE HOT ONE
(I LEAVE OUT THE WINE)

"THE HOT ONE"

Here's the adaptation from memory. It's easy to make and the flavor is good if you can overcome the misplaced fear of ruining your lobster. Don't let the Tabasco scare you. It's not too hot when you incorporate it into things.

The tools:

- Cutting board
- Cook's knife
- Skillet
- Whisk
- Tablespoon
- Garlic press
- Coffee mug/measuring cup

Here's what you need from the store:

- 1 onion
- Lobster base paste (you may substitute with chicken base)
- Flour
- Butter
- Eggs
- Tabasco
- Half & half (1 pint)
- 2 pounds lobster meat or meat from two steamed lobsters; tail & claw (or frozen tail meat)
- Parsley
- Paprika
- Long grain white rice

Here's how you put it together:

1. Steam your lobsters, cool them and then remove the meat. Set aside. (Or simply remove the meat from frozen lobster tails which have been cooked).

2. Turn the skillet to medium heat.

3. Chop half an onion and put it into the skillet with a half-stick of butter for 5 minutes on medium heat.

4. Add a teaspoon of lobster base paste and blend it in. (or use chicken base).

5. Add a tablespoon of flour and blend in with a whisk. ***Turn heat to medium-low.***

6. While stirring, slowly drizzle in a pint (or 2 mugs) of half & half, into which you have blended two egg yolks. Keep stirring until this becomes smooth and creamy. Add a little milk if you think it's too thick.

7. Add the lobster meat, cut into chunks.

8. Pour in one full tablespoon of Tabasco and blend well. Allow this to thicken as the lobster cooks.

9. Serve over mounds of hot, white rice. (See page 70).

10. Garnish with chopped fresh parsley sprinkled all around the rice.

11. Sprinkle a little paprika on top.

The strange origin of Lobster Thermidor

This spectacular creation was invented in 1894 at a Parisian restaurant, named Marie's, in honor of the opening of the stage play, "Thermidor" at a nearby theater. The play took its name from the midsummer month of the new French Republican Calendar of 1794.

It was during the month of Thermidor, on 27 July, 1794, that the infamous Robespierre, leader of the Reign of Terror in the French Revolution, was removed of his head by a guillotine.

He had been arrested by what used to be his own Committee of Public Safety; no doubt as a means of advancing the safety of the public by getting rid of Robespierre himself and his excessive blood lust.

This event became known as the Thermidorian Reaction (in which a revolutionary becomes seen as too radical even for his fellows and they get rid of him). Thus ending Robespierre's Reign of Terror right along with Robespierre himself.

Maximilien Robespierre

It wasn't Napoleon

A few have maintained that it was Napoleon who named lobster Thermidor because he allegedly first tasted it in the month of Thermidor, but this is extremely doubtful.

Napoleon had been friends with Robespierre's younger brother Augustin, and, during the Reign of Terror, was thrown into prison as a result of that association. Augustin's fate was to be executed by the same Committee which had dispatched his brother.

Napoleon was cleared a couple of weeks later and thence moved on to high rank in the army at the age of 27. He probably would not have mis-honored his late friend's downfall by naming a lobster dish after the event which caused his death, or, for that matter, naming anything good "Thermidor" so close to the signature event of Thermidor itself.

Besides, it would seem highly unlikely for anybody around that bloody time in Paris to be out dining anywhere on a fancy lobster dish, least of all one that carried the name associated with the very horrors going on all around them. You would not, for example, name something "Oysters Black Death" and expect it to remain a popular menu item during the plague.

LOBSTER THERMIDOR

The tools:

- 8-quart Boiling pot
- 2 cutting boards
- Cook's knife
- Whisk
- Strong scissors
- Teaspoon
- Tablespoon
- Kitchen tongs

It's OK if you cheat. You can forget the live lobsters and just get an equal amount of frozen lobster tails or meat. Complete steps 5 through 11 and then substitute any appropriate ramekins or small oven dishes for the empty shells.

Here's what you need from the store:

- 2 live lobsters @ 1.5 pounds*
- Unsalted butter
- 2 green onions
- Heavy cream (half pint)
- Eggs
- Coleman's English mustard
- Lemon
- Lobster base paste
- Grated Parmesan
- White wine
- Whole milk
- Sherry
- Nutmeg
- Parsley
- Paprika

Here's how you put it together:

1. Plunge the lobsters head-first into the pot of boiling, salted water.

2. After 8 to 10 minutes, remove the lobsters with the tongs and place them on a cutting board. Allow them to cool.

3. When cool enough to handle, use the strong scissors to cut each lobster down the back from head to tail, leaving the underside intact.

4. Get all the meat out of the claws and the tails and cut it into chunks. Set the meat aside and reserve the shells.

5. In a separate 1-quart pot, melt a half-stick of unsalted butter on low heat and add 3 Tablespoons of flour and mix well. Cook slowly for 3 minutes.

6. Add a teaspoon of the lobster base paste and blend.

7. Slowly drizzle in a mug of cream, stirring with a whisk the whole time. Let this cook WITHOUT BOILING for 3 minutes.

8. Add some salt, pepper and a little nutmeg.

9. In a separate pan, reduce a half mug of white wine and a quarter mug of sherry by half and then add this to the cream mixture.

10. Add 3 egg yolks and whisk over low heat 3 minutes.

11. Add a teaspoon of Coleman's Mustard and the lobster meat and stir well.

12. Spoon into the shells, top with some parmesan cheese, and broil 4 minutes.

The months of the French Republican Calendar are, in part:

Vendemiaire	"grape harvest"	(22 September to 21 October)
Brumaire	"fog"	(22 October to 20 November)
Frimaire	"frost"	(21 November to 20 December)
Nivose	"snowy"	(21 December to 19 January)
Pluviose	"rainy"	(20 January to 18 February)
Ventose	"windy"	(19 February to 20 March)
Germinal	"germination"	(21 March to 19 April) . . . etc.

And so on and on. Each of the days is numbered and is named after something familiar, such as "pigeon," "basil," or "oak." For example, the day they dragged old Robespierre down was on 27 Thermidor, also known as "rapeseed." This was thought to be an improvement. It wasn't. Napoleon abolished it in 1806. He left the metric system, however.

"WE'RE OFF TO SEE THE WIZARD"

The Republican Calendar was an expression of intellectual egoism which burgeoned in that period, marked by a compulsion to wipe the slate clean, to start everything at a new beginning, to overturn existing norms without worry about the consequences and to engineer humanity, culture, history, even time itself through science. For a number of these thinkers, science literally became the new religion, complete with "churches," priests and oaths to science. Science, or what most brainy people then imagined science was, suddenly became the benchmark for everything. Well, if it was the benchmark for everything, maybe you could predict the future. You could predict the future if you just added up all the scientific evidence about everything and extrapolated what seemed inevitable. Voila! Intellectuals never seem to give up on this idea because they're still at it.

"If you're so smart, why aren't you rich?"

This attempt to plan a new future without regard to the real-world, un-scientific consequences quickly morphed into socialism. That is what they called it. I'm just passing on the fact that they first gave it a name.

The new religion combining science, engineering, and a large quantum of hubris, started in France with the likes of Jean-Jacques Rousseau and others and was greatly elaborated upon in about 1817, by Henri de Saint-Simon, a failed aristocrat, knockabout and nere-do-well, who did a stint in the American Revolutionary Army as a teenager, dabbled in real estate ventures and engineering projects and lived the high life until he wound up penniless and dependent on others to support his grandiose schemes.

Partly thanks to his secretary, Auguste Comte, these "social science" ideas moved very rapidly into German universities and, along with virulent other "scientific" revolutionary ideas, became the clarion call for the collectivist redesign of humanity along the lines of tribalist conformity. It was avant garde; the very latest fashion statement. Intellectual goose-stepping by any other name is still goose-stepping.

By the time of the opening night of Thermidor, a hundred years had passed since Robespierre's head bit the dust. Karl Marx had already *been* dust for 11 years and the religious scientism of French and German eggheads became a yellow brick road to the future which many of us are still on, seeking the one behind the curtain who will save us with "the wonderful things he does."

MARENGO: A MORE PLAUSIBLE NAPOLEON FOOD STORY

On the late afternoon of June 14, 1800, Napoleon's forces won the Battle of Marengo, ultimately driving the opposing Austrian army out of Italy.

NAPOLEON BONAPARTE

This was the major battle of the Napoleonic wars, Waterloo notwithstanding. It was a long, hot, exhausting, bloody day, starting at six in the morning on the plains south of Turin, with musket and cannon fire slaughtering hundreds of men every few minutes. Napoleon had taken a reckless gamble and had stretched his line thin to anticipate the capture of the Austrian general, Michael von Melas, when Melas' infantry supposedly would be in retreat back to the north. This assumption may have been based on Napoleon's own high regard for his past successes and perhaps a sense of his own invulnerability.

However, Melas went viciously on the attack, routing the French by about one-thirty that afternoon. The French forces were beginning to fall back, still fighting but in growing disarray.

Earlier in the morning, as the opposing armies began to open fire, French Major General Louis Desaix, a trusted friend and confidant of Napoleon's, had been sent to flank the Austrians in the west, near Rivalta. Napoleon expected them to retreat and thereby be defeated when they, moving northward, encountered Desaix's force.

By mid-morning, however, things were not going according to expectations. Melas' attack was already taking a grave toll on the French troops, as were the heat and exhaustion. Many units were in retreat and under fire.

Desaix had already heard the cannon fire start up to the southeast and knew it was at Marengo. Without wasting a minute, he and his troops galloped off to join what he assumed was a major engagement. Halfway there he ran into an officer who had been hastily sent to recall him. Desaix and his men arrived at around three o'clock. When asked to give his estimation of the situation, he famously replied to Napoleon:

"This battle is completely lost. However there is still time to win another."

LOUIS DESAIX

With his three regiments, Desaix charged straight at Melas' center and overran the surprised and exhausted Austrian soldiers, winning victory from almost certain defeat. This was a huge loss for Austria and a stage-setting win for Napoleon.

It was during the climax of this battle that General Desaix was shot off his horse and killed by a musket ball. Napoleon later would order two monuments built to his memory.

I once stood beneath General Desaix's name on the Napoleon-inspired Arch de Triomphe and wondered what life had been like in those hazardous times and how much glory he or any of those fellows experienced while dying for the aims of an egomaniacal emperor who loved them so that he had their names chiseled in stone.

After Desaix's forces routed them, the Austrians had lost 6,000 men killed or wounded. The French 4,700. All in the space of 12 hours! History is full of such horrific clashes but it remains nearly impossible for us today to conceive of so many thousands of human beings being killed, face-to-face in less than 12 hours in one small place on the planet.

ARCH DU TRIOMPHE

"Dunand, serve up!"

Napoleon, who was as famous for his superstitious nature as for his tantrums, never ate anything before or during a battle, which meant that he usually was raving hungry at the conclusion of one.

At Marengo, it was no different. He told his chef, Dunand, to rustle up some grub immediately.

However, in the haste to engage the enemy, Napoleon's staff had rushed off without the supply wagon which held the provisions and utensils. And it was already getting dark.

Chef Dunand quickly went to nearby farms and foraged what he could. He returned with a chicken, some crawfish, tomatoes, onions, eggs, herbs, garlic, salt and a skillet. Then he cut up the chicken with a sword, worked some culinary magic on the rest and served it to his master, who loved it and ordered it served after every subsequent battle!

Apparently, the only ingredient that Dunand did not need to take from local farms was the brandy that he obtained from Napoleon's personal flask.

(You can have a sip of the general's favorite brandy if you get a bottle of Courvoisier. The label reads "cognac," the brandy that has long been made in that French city.)

CHICKEN MARENGO
Serves 4

The tools:

- Cutting board
- Cook's knife
- Large skillet with a lid (for the chicken)
- Medium skillet (for the mushrooms)
- Gallon ziplock bag
- Turning fork or tongs
- Holding plate
- Paper towels (for draining chicken)
- 4 small bowls
- Garlic press
- 2-quart pot
- Tablespoon
- Coffee mug
- Gallon-size ziplock bag

Here's what you need from the store:

- 2 chicken breasts
- 3 chicken thighs & 3 drumsticks
- Flour
- Butter
- Olive oil
- 2 Onions
- Garlic
- White wine
- Brandy
- 1-16-ounce can peeled, whole tomatoes (or 3 or 4 fresh, ripe tomatoes).
- Chicken base paste
- Fresh basil
- Fresh parsley
- Fresh mushrooms (sliced)
- Loaf of French Bread

Here's how you put it together:

1. Boil a bottle of white wine until it is reduced by half. Set aside.

2. Peel and slice (don't chop) the 2 onions and set aside in a small bowl.

3. Smash 3 cloves garlic and mix with the onions in the bowl.

4. Chop enough parsley and basil to get a handful of each and set this aside in another bowl.

5. Fry a couple of mugs full of the sliced mushrooms in olive oil, on high, just until golden and remove the browned slices to a small bowl.

6. Deglaze the hot skillet with a half-mug of brandy and then pour this over the mushrooms in the bowl. Turn heat to medium.

7. Season the cut up chicken pieces with Lawry's & pepper and shake them in a large ziplock bag with about a half a mug of the flour.

8. Fry the chicken pieces in about a half-inch of olive oil in the big skillet on medium heat until browned.

9. Remove the chicken to a plate and drain and cover with paper towels.

10. Drain the oil from the skillet.

11. In that same skillet on medium heat add the smashed garlic and onions for about 5 minutes then add the reduced white wine.

12. Add the tomatoes and a spoonful of the chicken base paste.

13. Add the basil, parsley & Tabasco and simmer for 15 minutes. Return the browned chicken pieces to the skillet, put the top on and allow to gently simmer on medium-low heat for 30 minutes.

14. Add the previously sauteed mushrooms to the chicken & tomato mixture and cook for 10 more minutes.

15. Serve with a basket of hot French bread.

This is a great little story, even if parts of it might by now have become muddled in history because it demonstrates what you can do with nothing more than what's on hand if you are resourceful. Not having stuff is a great way to acquire that discipline.

You can make this without adding the crawfish or the eggs (hard boiled or fried). Crawfish are delicious for use in Chicken Marengo but not strictly necessary.

You may favor a whole, cut-up chicken, cleaving the breasts pieces in half and separating the legs and thighs. It's also tolerable if you use skinned and boned breasts and thighs, so don't sweat it.

A little taste of history

Sticking to the original as closely as possible adds to a sense of capturing a bit of history. You can *really* capture history if you can eat it!

It's fun to sit at your table and reflect with your guests on the historical facts of the main course in front of them.

Incidentally, Napoleon's chef, Dunand, was the equally famous son of a well-known Swiss chef. After serving French military nobility for a decade, the son joined Napoleon and stuck with him until his master was exiled to the Island of St. Helena, where he received food barely worth eating. Napoleon gave Dunand his complete table service, which the old chef eventually left to the Museum of Lausanne, near his Swiss home.

Yet another Marengo

Napoleon obtained an Arabian horse after the Battle of Aboukir, in Egypt in 1799, which he rode during the Battle of Marengo and thence named "Marengo." This horse carried his master at Austerlitz in 1805, at Jena in 1806, at Wagram in 1809, during the Russian campaign in 1812 and at Waterloo in 1815. Chef Dunnand served his Chicken Marengo at the conclusion of every one of the battles involved. Marengo, the horse, was taken by the victors at Waterloo, and is now preserved in a lighted glass case at Britain's National Army Museum in London.

What county is this?

Twelve years after the crucial battle at Marengo, Napoleon and his Grand Army made the mistake of invading Russia, so damaging the French Army that it never recovered. Then, in 1813, the army was defeated at Leipzig and Napoleon was forced to abdicate. A number of people who were close to him were ordered to leave France by the king.

Those exiles were without a country until, in 1817, the U.S. Congress made land grants to them around what would become the river city of Demopolis, Alabama. The exiled settlers named their Alabama county Marengo.

Napoleon in Exile

"For what infamous treatment are we reserved! This is the anguish of death. To injustice and violence they now add insult and protracted torment. If I were so hateful to them why did they not get rid of me? A few musket balls in my heart or my head would have done the business and there would at least have been some energy in the crime."

Napoleon Bonaparte *in exile,*

Saint Helena Island, 1815

"Napoleon at Fontainebleau",
Paul Delaroche (1797-1856)
Musee de l'Armee, Paris

The painting by Delaroche captures Napoleon after the fall of Paris in March, 1814, before his first abdication. Here he seems to apprehend for the first time that his luck has run out. A year and a half later, he would be an exile on Saint Helena, where he died six years after his arrival there.

SPEAKING OF CRAWFISH . . . A TRIP TO CAJUN COUNTRY

Louisiana is the crawfish capitol of America, maybe the world, producing about 98 per cent of all the country's crawfish. Most of that harvest is consumed within Louisiana by a people famous for their love of great food, especially their long affection for crawfish.

Typically, these are boiled in a "tea" made of boiling water, lemons, oranges, bay leaves, onions, salt, red pepper and maybe a box of Zatarains Crab Boil and then removed to cool after a few minutes and eaten "as-is" without condiments (unless beer qualifies as a condiment).

SON, ROBERT, AT SAVY AUGUSTINE'S RICE PADDY NEAR MAMOU, LA --- ABOUT TO ADD HIS CATCH TO THE POT.

Beer: another of the main Cajun food groups?

Beer is widely recognized as being necessary at a Cajun crawfish boil. It's unlikely there ever was a Cajun crawfish boil without a lot of it on hand.

Typically, the cooked crawfish are drained and tossed onto a picnic table which has been covered with newspaper. Steaming mounds of dark red crawfish invite you to pig out on as many tails as you can "peel" before the next batch hits the table.

You also find "crawdads" baked in crawfish pie, stewed in crawfish gumbo or as the focal point in crawfish etouffee, one of the greatest gifts of the rice paddy and the bayou.

Any way you do crawfish, they are a delectable treat with a buttery taste suggestive of crab, shrimp and lobster combined. You can buy already shucked crawfish tails, freshly-packed or frozen. Both are good.

And if you want to put them in your Marengo for the sake of authenticity, remember that "authenticity" means they were most likely cooked in the original dish whole and eaten with the fingers, as Napoleon reportedly ate most of his food.

By summer, the shells get too hard to crack and the creatures lose some of their fat and flavor, although there is no actual crawfish "season."

All across Louisiana, you will find crawfish etouffee on the menu. If you order it you'll know why! You can also make it at home as follows:

CLAWLESS, COOKED CRAWFISH READY TO SHUCK (FOR ETOUFFEE GET THE TAIL MEAT ALREADY PEELED)

CRAWFISH ETOUFFEE

The tools:

- Cutting board
- Cook's knife
- Large skillet with a top
- Tablespoon
- Garlic press
- Coffee mug or cup

Here's what you need from the store:

- 2 pounds crawfish tail meat
- Celery
- 2 large onions
- Garlic
- Butter
- Green onions
- Jalapeno chiles
- Tabasco
- Bay leaves
- Red bell pepper
- Chicken base (*lobster base can overpower the crawfish flavors*).
- Parsley
- Flour
- Gravy Master
- Black pepper
- Paprika
- White rice

As of writing this, you can get five pounds of frozen Louisiana crawfish tail meat shipped to you for $90 from louisianaliving.com You may also be able to get the frozen tail meat at Sam's Club.

Here's how you put it together:

1. Chop 2 medium onions, 2 stalks celery, 1 seeded red bell pepper, 2 seeded jalapeno chiles. Smash 2 or 3 cloves of garlic. Set this aside in a bowl.

2. Chop 1/2 bunch of green onions, 1/2 bunch of parsley and set aside in a separate bowl.

3. Melt 1 stick of butter on medium heat in a large skillet that has a top and add the vegetables from the first bowl. Let this gently cook uncovered for 8 to 10 minutes.

4. Add the 2 pounds of thawed crawfish tails and the bay leaves, lower the heat to medium low and simmer for 10 minutes, stirring.

5. Blend a large teaspoonful of chicken base paste with an equal amount of flour & a few drops of water until smooth. Add this to the skillet.

6. Continuing to stir, add water a little at a time until the mixture is smooth and creamy-textured. Add a few drops of Gravy Master for a richer color.

7. Add the chopped green onions and parsley.

8. Add black pepper, Tabasco and paprika to taste, remove the bay leaves and cover with the heat turned off until ready to serve.

WHERE THE MEN ARE HOME ON THE RANGE

Calvin Trillin, New York writer and devotee of good food, once told of visiting Cajun country and of asking a friend in New Orleans beforehand for some good recommendations on where to eat when he got there.

"Eat anywhere," the friend advised him.

Cajuns take cooking so personally and are so serious and competitive about making it taste good that you really can eat just about anywhere and enjoy it whether it's a three star place with linen tablecloths or a filling station cafe with great boudin and red beans & rice.

Cajuns are long in the tradition of having good times and that typically centers around good food.

It's not uncommon to hear Cajuns at lunch talking about what they're making for supper or, for that matter, to be *preparing* supper as they're having lunch or even planning what they'll cook tomorrow!

There seems to be an unfortunate misperception in the part of the country that is not Louisiana that Cajun food is always "hot" or "spicy." This prejudice comes from cooks and chefs in the rest of the country, marketing their food as "Cajun" by the simple expedient of using too much cayenne and black pepper and trying to "blacken" everything.

The practice of "blackening," long common among African-Americans in the South, was popularized everywhere else by Cajun Chef Paul Prudhomme, the legendary, Louisiana chef who developed such a widespread following that "cajun" became the buzzword for making money in the restaurant, grocery and spice trades. His insistence on using redfish for blackening or court bouillon nearly wiped out the species because the chefs didn't know better.

There are companies now who package "blackening spices" so that you can blacken your food in the so-called Cajun manner, thereby supposedly lending it "authenticity."

But "authentic" is what you make it. Add-on spices are fine but real authenticity comes from the food components themselves, especially those that are native to the region.

Did You Know?

The word "Cajun" is a contraction of "Acadian" in the same way that "Injun" used to be a contraction of "Indian." Acadia was renamed Nova Scotia when the British kicked out the French settlers there who later migrated to Louisiana to become the Cajuns.

What makes Cajun food so distinctly good is not the red pepper or the application of mouth blistering "spicyness" but rather the heavy use of fresh local ingredients, crawfish being a great example, as well as the special love the people have for food, generally.

Also, there is a good likelihood that it's Cajun if the recipe tells you to *"start with a roux."*

Gumbo, Not Mumbo-Jumbo

If you haven't found out already, most of the gumbo served outside of New Orleans and the Cajun parishes of southwest Louisiana is mediocre or objectionable. This includes gumbo made from recipes that appear in magazines and on television. The problem is not that a lot of non-Cajun cooks and chefs actually *want* to make bad gumbo, they just don't get the medium and wind up making it complicated. Gumbo is very simple: *it's a roux that you add stuff to!*

If a guy doesn't have a clue what "file" is, he shouldn't put it in his gumbo. And if he does, he shouldn't also use okra. And if he does use okra he needs to know how to use it without making it slimy. You can avoid using either one of these ingredients but if you do use okra, caramelize the slices first, otherwise your gumbo may turn out to be slimy.

Savy Augustine, my Mamou buddy, drove me over to his fish camp on a small lake one afternoon to join the Deshotel twin brothers, Ed and Bee, along with Hadley Fontenot and a fresh bottle of Jack Daniels.

These men, French-speaking cowboys and farmers to a man, were widely recognized as some of the best Cajun musicians in Louisiana and my hope that they were bringing instruments was rewarded by an unbelievable afternoon of picking, playing, drinking and singing Cajun music.

I also learned from Savy the main thing about making a good gumbo:

"It's a roux you add stuff to, Bob."

Savy's wife, Clarisse, was an excellent cook and they taught me to make a gumbo that might even pass muster in Mamou. That's a qualified "might even" but I'll let Mamou be the judge.

The key really is the roux. This is one of the reasons that gumbo becomes much more than the sum of its parts because its parts consist basically of vegetables, meat, flour and oil. The application of heat and patience to these ingredients can make a proper foundation for many Creole and Cajun dishes, especially including gumbo. And don't worry about using a lot of oil for the roux. You can skim it off the top later on if you want to.

Gumbo is one of those warming foods that soothes the heart and mind. If it doesn't cheer you up, you probably need more than mere food.

Chicken & Sausage Gumbo

Serves 8-10

People who taste gumbo for the first time express wonderment about where the amazing flavor comes from and will ask you what special seasonings were used. But this distinctive taste comes from the dark roux. Your roux is perfect when it is approximately the color of melted milk chocolate.

The tools:

- Cutting board
- Cook's knife
- Large bowl
- 6-quart pot
- Coffee mug/cup
- Whisk
- Tablespoon
- Garlic press

Here's what you need from the store:

- Celery
- 2 onions
- Garlic
- Green onions
- Parsley
- Red bell pepper
- 2 or 3 jalapeno chiles
- Dried bay leaves
- Chicken thighs
- Kielbassa (or smoked sausage)
- Andouille* (if you like)
- Gravy Master
- Tabasco
- Black pepper
- Chicken base paste
- Peanut oil
- Flour

* (andouille is a type of garlicky French or Cajun sausage containing hot spices and lots of garlic).

You want to have all of your stuff out and gathered together before you get started.

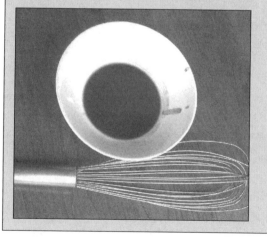

This should be the approximate shade of your roux when it's ready. This one took me 30 minutes of constant whisking to reach this stage. This is just a small sample of that batch. A good roux is well worth the effort!

Here's how you put it together:

1. Chop 2 onions, 4 ribs of celery, 1 half bunch of parsley, 1 bunch of green onions, 3 or 4 seeded jalapeno chiles, 1 red bell pepper and 2 or 3 cloves of garlic and set aside in a big bowl.

2. Pour 3/4 mugful of oil into the 6-quart pot, add 3/4 mugful of flour, turn the heat to medium* and start stirring this constantly with a whisk.

3. When the roux is dark enough and still hot, dump all the chopped vegetables in and stir well.

4. When the vegetables are soft add 2 quarts of water.

5. Add 2 Tablespoons chicken base paste (you can add more later if needed).

6. Add 1 tablespoon of Gravy Master.

7. Add 3 or 4 bay leaves and as much black pepper as you like.

8. Allow the pot to simmer for 1 hour then add 1.5 pounds kielbasa cut to 1-inch lengths. (Also add about a quarter-pound of andouille if you want).

9. Add 6 or 8 skinned chicken thighs (you can leave the bones in).

10. Add more water if needed and allow to simmer for another 90 minutes

11. Serve around a mound of hot, white rice. (But not par-boiled rice!)

Note: When making roux, you must stir constantly and not divert your attention or walk away, even for a moment! Inattention could result in burnt roux, which CANNOT be salvaged. It must be discarded and you have to start all over again.

Roux is also known as "cajun napalm," as it sticks readily to most surfaces can cause first and second degree burns. Be VERY careful not to get any on yourself!

Some call this "prairie gumbo" because it is typical of the rice farming and cattle raising parishes where my friends live.

Farther to the south, along the swampy bayous and coastal areas, the seafood version is the rule. If you'd like a seafood gumbo, it's much the same thing although you will need to make a seafood stock to use with your chicken (base paste) stock. I find that the chicken base works fine as a supplement to the stock that you make.

COSTUMED RIDERS MAKING THE MARDI GRAS CIRCUIT AROUND MAMOU. THEY DO THIS ALL DAY AND RIDE BACK INTO TOWN AT DUSK, IN TIME FOR GUMBO AND THE ALL-NIGHT DANCE.

If you do make your own stock, use the shells from two pounds of shrimp and fish scraps and all of your vegetable trimmings in about a half-gallon of water, slowly boil it down to less than a quart and strain it off (you will put the peeled shrimp in the gumbo).

Instead of chicken, duck or sausage, seafood gumbo includes crab, shrimp, fish filets and freshly shucked oysters. Many cooks just chop the crabs in half and throw them in the gumbo, shells and all. Add the cut fish filets last so that they don't disintegrate with too much cooking.

If you have a good seafood market nearby, ask them if you can get any fresh fish trimmings or "fish bones" and add some (heads and tails) to the stockpot. The richer you make the stock, the better the flavor of the end result.

Also, see if you can find head-on shrimp. The heads and shells combined make the best stock.

It is best to stay away from mushrooms, wine reductions and tomatoes and limit the fresh herbs to curly leaf parsley. You don't need shallots either but green onions are an absolute necessity. When Cajuns refer to green onions, they just say "onion tops" because the white bottoms don't add much.

This particular gumbo is a staple in all the Cajun parishes of southwest Louisiana.

Another basic, one-course meal is red beans and rice and you'll find this everywhere in Louisiana, and even well beyond Cajun country.

Many places in downtown New Orleans feature red beans and rice for lunch, traditionally on Monday, and you're likely to see mud-caked pipeline construction workers sitting next to bankers in suits, happily munching red beans and rice from steaming plates garnished with smoked sausage, chopped green onion and buttered french bread toast.

"Good" has no class status or distinction but it has fans from across the entire cultural spectrum.

RED BEANS & RICE

Serves 4-6

The tools:
- Colander
- 4-quart bowl or
- 2-quart pitcher
- Cutting board
- Cook's knife
- Garlic press
- 6-quart pot

Here's what you need from the store:
- 1-pound package of dried red beans
- Bacon
- Garlic
- 1 softball-sized onion
- 3 or 4 jalapeno chiles
- A small ham hock (or get the butcher to cut a big one in half) or just add more bacon.
- Chicken base paste and Gravy Master
- Celery
- Parsley
- Bay leaves
- Kielbassa (2 lb.)
- Green onions
- Tabasco

Here's how you put it together:

Rinse in a colander, remove debris and soak the beans overnight in the refrigerator in enough water to cover. (You may need to add a little more water later, as the beans do absorb it readily).

The next day:

1. Rinse the beans in the colander again.

2. Cut up 6-8 slices of bacon and fry in the 6-quart pot.*

3. Add chopped onion, 4 ribs of chopped celery & 3 or 4 seeded, chopped jalapenos, 2 cloves smashed garlic, half-bunch chopped green onion and stir until softened.

4. Add the beans, 3 quarts water and a teaspoon of Gravy Master.

6. Add the Ham hock.

7. Add 2 tablespoons chicken base paste (you will test for saltiness later).

8. Add 4 or 5 bay leaves. Allow this to slowly simmer for 2 hours, then add the cut up sausages & more green onions and simmer another hour or so. Serve, garnished with chopped fresh green onion.

(Freeze the strips of bacon first and then you can easily chop them into small bits on your cutting board. Allow the bits to cook slowly until they are uniformly crisp).

For perfect rice:

Put a coffee mug of raw rice in a 2-quart pot that has a lid. Add slightly less than 2 coffee mugs of water and about a half-teaspoon of salt and some black pepper. Add some butter. Bring the pot to a boil on high and then **immediately** turn heat to **low** and cover the pot. DO NOT UNCOVER THE POT! Allow rice to cook for 15 minutes then turn off heat and leave the pot alone. In 5 minutes you'll have your perfect rice. (Don't cheat by lifting the lid to peek at the rice because you will negate part of the steaming/absorption process). The rice should be slightly "sticky."

STEAMED RICE
IMAGE COURTESY OF LIVESTRONG.COM

Notes _____

_____

_____

_____

_____

_____

_____

_____

_____

_____

_____

_____

_____

_____

_____

_____

_____

_____

_____

_____

_____

_____

_____

_____

_____

_____

MELROSE - AN ANTEBELLUM HOME, NATCHEZ, MISSISSIPPI
IMAGE COURTESY OF WIKIPEDIA, TAKEN BY R. STEPHENS

Soulful & Southern

CHARLES EVERS, MARCHING FROM NATCHEZ TO FAYETTE, MISSISSIPPI, AS THAT TOWN'S NEW MAYOR

NIGHT MOVES

Back in the early Seventies, during the civil rights wars; before reporters turned into "journalists" and even before professors were hippies or hippies were politicians, it became my privilege to run around Mississippi with Charles Evers, famed leader of black people in that state, whose brother Medgar had recently been assassinated. The klan was continuing their murderous hobby of dynamiting the homes of people that they didn't like, regardless of race. We felt several of these blasts rumble through the house from various white neighborhoods around town, sort of like little earthquakes. It was always late at night.

Evers almost single handedly had kept the city of Jackson from the wrath of angry black mobs at the height of the Jackson State University riots. He took a megaphone and told them not to hate and he changed their minds and hearts one afternoon from the steps of the courthouse downtown.

That event was covered on the local evening news and it affected me. Jackson had just dodged a bullet, thanks to Evers' commanding presence and his exhortations to non-violence.

I took off work early the next day and went over to Evers' office on Lynch Street to thank him. I told him I'd like to write a magazine article about him and his work in Mississippi.

"I'm goin' to Brookhaven tonight. We havin' a meetin'. Wanna go?"

Out of the blue! Just like that!

Before I could think or consider the ramifications, I said I did and then called my wife, who told me a couple of times that I had lost my mind and not to blame her if I got shot.

One of the best things I remember about Evers then, apart from his leadership quality, was his sense of humor. Despite the awful seriousness of the fight he was waging, he was one funny individual. It was part of his makeup. He loved irony.

The meeting was in a church. It was hot and the ladies were busy fanning themselves. Before Evers got up to speak, they all started singing a hymn --- no books, no piano, no choir director, no choir. The hymn was "Amazing Grace." Everybody in the whole church just started singing this amazingly beautiful song, completely a'capella with what sounded like eighteen-part harmony. It was like nothing I had ever heard. Afterwards, Evers told them to avoid local businesses that were involved with the Klan. He also reminded them to avoid hating anybody.

"Let the klukkers hate," he said, "they ain't go'n win this fight but we go'n lose it if we ourselves go to hatin'."

He once asked me to drive the two of us from a night meeting in Natchez, 85 miles back to Jackson. I said sure, without considering how else I could get there.

I bought a six pack of Budweiser and had it on the front seat between us. He had a loaded .30 caliber military carbine propped against the seat. He also had a .45 ACP loaded in the glove compartment and a loaded .38 Special revolver tucked into his belt. I didn't have anything besides the beer and that included not having any ice.

I eased us out of Natchez around midnight. A few minutes later we were on a two-lane blacktop road through a darkened wilderness of live-oak limbs draped in Spanish moss. He told me to speed up. Speed up!

"I'm already going the speed limit," I protested.

"I can see that," he said, "but I don't want no headlights in the rear view. Speed on up."

I pushed the car to seventy and glanced over at Evers, who was pretending to go to sleep, the dim glow from the dashboard lights revealing one partially open eye. I told myself that there was no reason to get scared. However, on reflection, there may have been a couple. I reached into my little brown sack and got a beer. Courage was just a can or two away.

"Heh, heh."

"What?"

"They go'n put you an' me both under the jail they catch us; you drinkin' and me colored. Heh, heh. They go'n say 'Hey look'a here boys! We done got us a drunk drivin' white boy and ol' Evers here an' a bunch'a guns. Let's run 'em in and throw away the key!'." Pause.

"Ain't you 'fraid 'a being caught drinkin'? An' speedin', too!"

"No. I'm afraid of being caught driving you to Jackson."

"Heh, heh. Why don't you set yo'self lower in the seat?"

But I already had done that.

In those tumultuous years, Evers and I became friends. The klan knew it too, from "evidence" they picked up at the main post office, which included the picture on a previous page that I had mailed out for processing.

Every week or two some of them would park a car in front of my house, turn off the headlights and just quietly sit there. Three or four guys would be inside and they would smoke with the parking lights on for an hour or so. Then they would slowly, silently drive away, turning the headlights back on halfway down the street.

The klan gives up the ghost

It isn't clear exactly what straw finally broke the klan's back in Mississippi, but there was such a rapid accumulation of deadly, klan-caused events in those years that people across the state got fed up and juries, some of them mostly-white, started putting those people away. Trials started ending with klansmen being convicted and sent to jail.

Once public opinion had reached that point, the klan no longer had "cover" and it was finally over. Cowards fight when they think the public is so afraid of them that not enough of the public will stick their necks out in opposition. But the necks were out in force.

I once asked Evers if he would call E.L. McDaniel, Imperial Wizard of the Mississippi Klan, and offer to sit down with him and have a rational discussion (with me allowed in the room, taking notes).

"Hell, I already made that clear," he told me.

"He knows what we doin' and he knows he don't stand a chance so he's scared a' talkin'. He's scared a' US! They ALL scared."

Pause.

"They ain't go'n be no kluckkers here one day."

Sweet tea, grits, turnip greens & fried chicken; four of the 100 major southern food groups

Evers owned a restaurant in Fayette, Mississippi, where he was mayor and we would eat there if we were in town near lunchtime.

At Ever's place you enjoyed the typical Southern fare of turnip greens, sweet potatoes, fresh lima beans or sugar peas, cornbread or biscuits with chicken gravy and heaps of fried chicken or maybe fried catfish and hush puppies with gallons of freshly made, sweet iced tea. All of this would be accompanied by the music of B.B. King, Eretha Franklin or The Supremes on the jukebox and followed by a bowl of cold, banana pudding and some more sweet tea.

"Come on! You eatin' like a bird!"

"I'm stuffed."

"Naw, seriously. Get some more. You didn't even try the pork chops."

"I'm sure they're great, Charlie, but if I eat anything else I'm going to drop dead."

"Heh, heh."

A simple way to make fried chicken

Alex Waites, a civil rights lawyer and friend of Evers, told me one day how his mother made fried chicken by "steam-frying" it. We were forced to miss lunch on the way to Natchez, and his telling of her method made us all hungry. The concept was interesting enough to try at home and, in fact, resulted in the best fried chicken I had ever made. There are ways you might complicate this but why would you want to do that? After many trials and errors, the following plan evolved, based on a combination of frying and steaming at the same time.

ALEX WAITES'S MOTHER'S
STEAM-FRIED CHICKEN

The tools:

- Cutting board
- Cook's knife
- Gallon ziplock bag
- Garlic press
- Coffee mug/measuring cup
- Large skillet with a lid
- Tablespoon
- Paper towels

Here's what you need from the store:

- 4 each, chicken thighs & legs (bone-in)
- 2 chicken breasts (bone in)
- Garlic
- Lawry's Seasoned Salt
- Black pepper
- Cayenne (red) pepper if you want
- Flour for dredging
- Gallon sized ziplock bags
- Peanut oil

Here's how you put it together:

1. Remove the skin and chop the breasts pieces in half crosswise. (rock your cook's knife to & fro and bear down real hard with the heel of your hand).

2. Remove the skin from the legs & thighs if you want to.

3. Rinse and dry the chicken pieces (with paper towels).

4. Rub with smashed garlic, Lawry's seasoned salt & black pepper.

5. Shake all the pieces in a ziplock bag with enough flour to coat well.

6. Pour a mugful or more of the oil into a large skillet (the oil should be about 1/4 inch deep). Then turn the heat to high.

7. After one minute, turn the heat to medium and carefully put the coated chicken pieces in the skillet.

8. Turn all the pieces after 2 minutes then cover the skillet and turn the heat to low.

9. Keep turning and re-covering the chicken pieces every few minutes for about 20 to 30 minutes on low heat until the pieces are golden all over and the meat starts to feel loose on the bone.

10. Drain on paper towels and serve hot.

Gently frying the chicken on low heat while covered keeps the moisture inside the skillet and thus inside the chicken. This "steams" the chicken while it is frying. Don't rush it.

NOW FOR A LITTLE GRAVY

When you make fried chicken you might want to serve it with rice. One of the best things for rice is gravy. You already know how to make perfect rice (page 70). Here is a simple plan for making gravy.

1. Drain the oil from your skillet but do not scrape it clean. Leave some of the toasted flour in there.

2. Pour a couple of tablespoons of fresh, new olive oil into the center of the skillet.

3. Turn the heat to medium.

4. Add a teaspoon or two of flour and blend well with a whisk

5. Add a teaspoon of chicken base paste and blend well.

6. As the mixture starts to heat up, slowly pour in a mug of water while constantly blending with the whisk so that you deglaze the skillet at the same time.

7. Allow this to cook for about a minute until creamy and smooth.

8. Add 1 teaspoon of Gravy Master (or more as desired for darkened color) and whisk it in.

9. Add as much black pepper as you want (& more water if thinning is needed).

GOOD GRAVY, GOOD RICE

You also can use half & half for a richer gravy. For all-around appeal, the best rice is regular, long grain rice that you find on the store shelf, such as Carolina Rice, River Rice and others.

Texmati white rice may be the best tasting rice but it is expensive. This is a domesticated cross between Texas long grain rice and Indian basmati. This variety is also grown in Cajun country (Ellis Stansel Rice: see www.cajungrocer.com).

Coffee & donuts with Robert E. Lee

I asked Evers to come in the house before he went home one late night. My wife was waiting up and wanted to meet him and had made coffee.

"Naw," I can't come in your house," he said, "the kluckkers could be watchin' and your neighbors might object. You could get in trouble." I told him that we had coffee and donuts and my wife was expecting us. He finally agreed.

As he sat at our table in the small dining room, I realized that he was sitting directly beneath a framed picture on the wall of General Robert E. Lee, given to me by my grandmother. I asked him to turn around and see who was on the wall. He looked at that picture of Lee for a few seconds then turned back to the coffee.

"He was a fine man, General Lee," he said. "He stood up for black people when nobody else would. He was never unkind to our people."

Evers saw through people instantly, with the legendary genius of a horse or a child and if they were phony or deceitful he knew it and knew exactly how to deal with them: bluntly and with the power of unassailable logic and force of character. You couldn't get anything past him. I am convinced that this is why he invited me to ride with him on that first occasion without verifying that I was who I said I was. He *knew!*

"We all grew up here," he told me one time, "and it don't matter what's the color of our skin. Deep down we all need one another and we better get along 'cause they ain't no other way. Ain't never go'n *be* no other way, neither."

We were fortunate to have been in the middle of all that. Those were exciting times and events. The culture of Mississippi went through a painful realignment without losing itself in revolt, thanks largely to the courage and sheer force of will represented by Charles Evers.

GENERAL ROBERT E. LEE

The power of one

It was Evers, more than anyone else, who stared down both the Ku Klux Klan and the hot-headed Mau Maus who wanted fire, revenge and bloodshed. He let both camps know that they could get their butts kicked. He differed markedly from Martin Luther King but achieved the same result without violence.

There was a definite element of fear that Evers inspired in people in those days. Nobody wanted to cross him because there was always an unspoken threat that if they did cross him they could face unpleasant consequences. Violence was never used but you didn't want to tempt fate by poking a tiger with a stick.

Elegant grits

The image of grits as lowbrow food comes from their cheap abundance across most of the South. In the period after the devastation of the Civil War, people in the region struggled, many on what would have been subsistence diets had it not been for corn grits. Corn is a grass and grows as quickly as grass.

The corn produced in a season can not be consumed by animals and humans all at once so it has to be stored someplace and that place needs to be near a river, a road or a railroad if you're ever to get it to market.

The best way to store corn when there aren't any of the above, is by converting it into whiskey. However, there's a problem. After George Washington and the American Army ended the Whiskey Rebellion in 1794, in Western Pennsylvania, you had to lay pretty low if you wanted to store your corn crop in jars, so grits became an ideal way to put aside corn for future food use without running from the revenuers.

Much of the grits served in the South is not the old-fashioned, stone ground and highly flavorful corn porridge of yesteryear. That is increasingly hard to find because it can go bad after a year on the shelf.

Grits are so much taken for granted now that a lot of restaurants just boil up pots of "instant" grits, a genuine abomination. This is bad because it gives grits a terrible reputation which is only reinforced by the next encounter with them at any place that considers grits as just a plate-filler.

A lot northerners are thus understandably put off by grits and make grits an object of ridicule. Yet the same people can love eating entire bowls of popcorn and apparently have affection for corn muffins, neither of which has the rich corn flavor of good, old-fashioned, slow-cooked, stone-ground grits.

Fortunately, there is a delightful and elegant way to serve grits and it is a crowd pleaser even in the North although not so much for breakfast. Here it is:

"An inexpensive, simple and thoroughly digestible food, grits should be made popular throughout the world. Given enough of it, the inhabitants of Planet Earth would have nothing to fight about. A man full of grits is a man of peace."

– Charleston Post & Courier

SIMPLE CHEESE GRITS

Serves 8 as a side dish

The tools:

- 3-quart pot with lid
- Large bowl
- Coffee mug/measuring cup
- Tablespoon
- Whisk
- 3-quart baking dish (9" X 12" X 3")

Here's what you need from the store:

- White or yellow corn grits, preferably stone ground (www.oakviewfarms.com)
- Unsalted butter
- Chicken base paste
- 1 Half-pint of half & half
- Eggs
- Grated mild yellow cheddar cheese

Here's how you put it together:

1. Bring 3 cups of water to a boil
2. Add a mounded tablespoon of chicken base paste (replaces salt)
3. Whisk the grits in and turn heat to low.
4. Cook on low for 15 minutes, stirring occasionally.
5. Remove from heat. Let stand covered for 5 minutes.
6. Put into a large bowl along with half a stick of butter, 2 handfuls of the cheese and 4 large, beaten eggs.
7. Sprinkle the top with some cheese.
8. Bake at 350 degrees for 45 minutes.
9. Allow to "rest" for 10 minutes before serving.

Shrimp & Grits

This originated as a breakfast dish along the rivers and estuaries of the coastal Carolinas and has long been a favorite of the locals.

However, it was simply too good tasting to be avoided by chefs at upscale restaurants, who saw it as much more than breakfast fare. Today, you can find shrimp 'n grits everywhere from Charleston to San Francisco.

I had a fabulous version of it for lunch in Columbia, SC. The chef there made his with yellow grits instead of the more common white variety.

At a restaurant in Calistoga, CA, the young chef served grits as an evening dish; pouring the hot grits cooked in chicken stock into a shallow baking pan and then cutting the cool sheet into rounds about three quarters of an inch thick. She then fried these in butter until golden brown on both sides and served them under a rich sauce, loaded with shrimp.

LADLE YOUR SHRIMP WITH ITS "GRAVY" ON TOP OF A LARGE MOUND OF HOT GRITS

SHRIMP & GRITS

Serves 2

The tools:

- Skillet
- Garlic press
- Cutting board
- Cook's knife
- 3-quart pot with a lid
- Tablespoon
- Teaspoon
- Coffee mug
- Bowl

Here's what you need from the store:

- 1-pound raw shrimp
- Bacon
- Garlic
- Green onions
- Jalapenos & red bell pepper
- Olive oil
- White wine
- Fresh basil
- 1 pint cream
- White or yellow corn grits
- Butter
- Chicken base paste
- 1 pound pack grated mild yellow cheddar cheese
- Black pepper
- Tabasco
- 1 medium tomato (optional)

Here's how you put it together:

FOR THE GRITS:

1. Mix 2 1/4 mugs of water with 2 teaspoons of chicken base in a lidded 3-quart pot.

2. Add a quarter-stick of butter and bring to a boil.

3. Whisk in a half-cup of the grits stirring constantly then immediately reduce heat to low and cover.

4. Stir every 4 minutes, making sure the grits don't stick to the bottom.

5. After 15 minutes, remove pot from the heat, whisk in half a mug of cream and cover.

FOR THE SHRIMP:

1. Fry 5 or 6 slices of bacon in the skillet on medium-low heat until crisp. Remove.

2. Chop 2 or 3 green onions, 1 red bell pepper,two seeded jalapeno chiles. Set aside.

3. Chop a small handful of fresh basil.

4. Remove bacon and press dry with paper towels, leaving the drippings in the skillet.

5. Add chopped vegetables to the skillet, with heat on medium, and cook for 6 minutes.

6. Add the raw, peeled shrimp and stir this for 5 minutes.

7. Add the bacon, crumbled.

8. Pour in a half-mug of white wine and allow this to simmer for 1 minute.

9. Add a pint of cream.

10. Add black pepper & Tabasco as desired.

11. *OPTIONAL:* fold in fresh cut tomato pieces if desired.

SHRIMP TALES

Growing up less than 200 miles from the Gulf of Mexico is a fortunate confluence of geography and family history which can result in memories that have lasting appeal: of getting up before the sun and having breakfast on the way down to the beach, usually at a shabby roadside joint that had terrific food; of the snow-white sand and clear ocean water; of chasing sand crabs at night in the light of the moon and the wonderful sensation of diving into cool surf with a case of sunburn and getting blissfully swift, cool relief.

Those are the fond childhood memories. Spring break came later and created a host of its own fond recollections.

What you did a lot of, regardless of age or inclination, was boil shrimp and then chill them down in tubs of ice and eat your fill. You'd peel them and dip them in your own special concoction of chili sauce, fresh lemon, Tabasco, "wooster" sauce, horseradish and realize that it was just possibly the best thing you'd ever tasted.

EARLY JULY MORNING, FLORIDA GULF OF MEXICO

The shrimp were nearly as good hot, too, dipped in melted butter and splashed with some Tabasco and wrapped up in a piece of hot, crusty French bread. It's almost as good as lobster.

The secret to good boiled shrimp is to make the right brew for cooking. The best boiling mix on the market is probably Zatarains. They've been making their crab boil in New Orleans for well over a century. You can add a little to it as follows:

SHRIMP BOIL

Bring two or three of gallons of water to a boil and throw in a bag of Zatrain's (It comes in a little, perforated bag inside its box so that you don't have to rinse the shrimp of the seeds and flakes). Then add a couple of cut up oranges or lemons, a couple of quartered onions and a half box of salt and let it slowly boil for about half an hour. Then toss in 4 pounds of shrimp.

This same plan can be used with lobster, crab and crawfish.

Let the "tea" containing the shrimp come back to a boil and then simmer for 10 minutes more before removing to drain. Cover with ice. When cool enough to handle, start peeling and eating. Re-use the old boiling water for the next batch.

Like the smell of the surf itself, the salty aromas of boiling shrimp can remind you of the ocean even when you are away from the beach.

Sometimes at night you would sit out on the dunes and stare at the horizon and let your thoughts wander out over the waves and share the sounds and the warm air with friends.

Today, the Gulf of Mexico is home to a dwindling but still significant shrimp fleet, supplying the country with 12 percent of its wild-caught shrimp. The other 88 per cent comes from Thailand, Indonesia, Vietnam and China, where fisheries are exploited by those taking advantage of ecosystems without following rules. In other words, they farm the shrimp and have used bottom dredges which tear up the mangroves that provide habitat.

Gulf shrimpers are now having their product clearly marked as domestic wild caught and you can see that on their labels in the store.

Shrimp Newberg

This super-rich concoction started out as Lobster Newberg at Delmonico's in New York in 1876. A rich sea captain named Ben Wenburg, showed proprietor Charles Delmonico how to make a lobster-cream dish so Delmonico, who was impressed by it, put it on his menu and named it after Ben.

Some months later, these two had an argument and Delmonico took "Lobster Wenburg" off the menu. He told Ben not to come back. However, his customers kept asking for it so he changed the name (swapping the "W" and the "N") to Lobster Newberg and it stuck.

Today, Delmonico's in New York still features "1876 Lobster Newburg" on the menu for $49 and just beneath the listing is *"Sauce a' la Wenberg,"* apparently return-ing some credit belatedly back to old Ben.

Lobster can be expensive, however, so the same dish may be made using shrimp or a combination of shrimp and any firm crabmeat. It is still good and you will have enough money left over to pick up a couple of bottles of wine.

Incidentally, Delmonico's also claims not only to be the first true fine dining res-taurant in America but the inventor of the American hamburger and eggs benedict as well. In 1876, American fine dining was limited to the better hotels until Delmonico's blazed the trail.

You can substitute jumbo lump crabmeat for the shrimp but then one might ask "why not just go with the lobster?" However, if you do use crab, fold it in gently.

SHRIMP NEWBERG

Serves 4

The tools:

- Skillet
- Teaspoon
- Whisk
- Coffee mug/cup
- 4-quart bowl
- Pot with lid for the rice
- Jigger

Here's what you need from the store:

- Unsalted butter
- Flour
- Cayenne pepper
- Nutmeg
- 1 pint cream
- Sherry
- Eggs
- Tabasco
- Lobster base paste
- 2 pounds raw shrimp
- Long grain white rice or frozen puff pastry shells

Here's how you put it together:

1. Peel the shrimp, saute it in a little oil while stirring for 5 minutes. Set aside.
2. Melt a half-stick of butter in another saucepan over medium-low heat.
3. With a whisk, blend in 2 Tablespoons of the flour.
4. Add a little cayenne pepper and nutmeg.
5. Blend in 1 spoonful of lobster base paste (should replace the salt).
6. Slowly, while whisking, add a pint of cream and then a couple jiggers of sherry and a full teaspoon of Tabasco. Turn heat to low.
7. Cook this until it is thickened and smooth, about a minute
8. Pour half of this mixture into a bowl and then whisk in 3 egg yolks. Add the egg yolk mixture back to the sauce and whisk it in.
9. Add the shrimp and cook for 2 more minutes. (Do not overcook).

Speaking of Delmonico's . . .
Just what is a Delmonico steak?

The answer is, nobody knows anymore. Meat enthusiasts speculate that it is one of eight known cuts, ranging from a chuck eye steak to any bone-in ribeye to any bone-in top loin. The chuck eye steak is interesting because there are only two of them per beef. Is that it? We don't know.

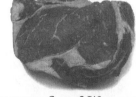

The archaeology of this steak is different from that of ancient tombs in that ancient tombs actually contain sufficient, tangible clues for the archaeologist to learn from. In this case all of the original Delmonico steaks are long washed off the plate and apparently nobody at the time thought to write down exactly what the cut was.

Delmonico Steak? Who knows?

The original Delmonico's lasted 96 years in New York, at one time having four locations in the city under family management. Its reputation grew to prominence everywhere that people respected good food, especially food which was presented in the European (French) manner. Did they leave a clue? No.

Many people assume that a proper Delmonico (sometimes called a "club" steak) is a kind of thick-cut ribeye. However, I find ribeye steaks, at least those not pared down to the central "filet," to be a dishevelled mess to contend with on a plate.

You can't go wrong with a New York strip, a Porterhouse or its first cousin, the T-bone. These have the flavor that good steak ought to have and the additional advantage of being easy to work with. And you don't even need a grill.

Delmonico's done in by the moral crusade

Sadly, the original Delmonico's ceased to exist in 1920, when, with a foresight peculiar to zealots, anti-booze puritans got up off their knees and went into the world of sin to change human nature. They failed at that but they got Prohibition passed into law.

There was no more great wine in the cellar (they sold it all to wealthy patrons who started entertaining at home), there was no more rum or brandy or sherry for cooking, no more red wine reductions for demi glazes. And there was no more fun sitting at your table enjoying three or four hours of wonderful food with a cordial drink or two. All gone. Today, who can foresee the results of prohibiting salt or cooking oils? Will there be French fry speakeasies? Crisco bootleggers busting the blockades? Revenuers chasing armed salt runners through the woods? A Salt Mafia?

Some of the famous patrons of Delmonico's in past years have Included England's King Edward VII, Theodore Roosevelt and Mark Twain.

GREAT STEAK WITHOUT THE GRILL

Sometimes you can learn more by making a mistake, which is to say you can become good at something by initially failing at it. This seems to be the rule. There are exceptions. There is no use learning algebra, for example, no matter how many times you fail it in school. It is useless information. Let it so remain.

HOW TO COOK A STEAK IN A SKILLET
(Virtually as good as grilling):

1. Smash some garlic and rub the juice all over the steaks. (Leave the fat on.)
2. Sprinkle both sides and the edges with Lawry's Seasoned Salt. Rub it in.
3. Sprinkle with black pepper. Rub it in.
4. Turn a skillet to high heat. Wait about a three minutes.
5. Lay your steak in (it should be cut 1" thick) immediately turn the heat to medium.
6. Cook on medium for 5 minutes.
7. Then turn the steak over.
8. Immediately turn the heat off. Put some butter on the steak.
9. Wait 4 minutes.
10. Serve with the darkest side up which should be the side that hit the heat first.

Drizzle with any butter left in the skillet or deglaze with a small amount of water, salt & butter. Serve with a nice helping of "Mushrooms and Sour Cream" (next page).

The difference between a porterhouse and a T-bone is the section of the loin from which they're cut. Both are comprised of two, distinct sections separated by a bone, one section being the "strip" from which NY strips are trimmed and the other being the filet or part of the meat that produces fillet mignon.

This picture shows you a porterhouse steak on the left and a T-Bone on the right. The minor difference is that the porterhouse has more of the fillet and the T-bone has a more well defined strip. Either way, you're getting both a strip steak and a fillet mignon in one package. The porterhouse steak, reputedly was originally served at Martin Morrison's Porter House at 327 Pearl Street in Manhattan. Either steak is wonderfully accompanied by mushrooms Romanov.

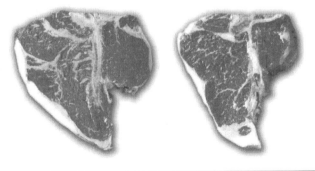

In 1933, when my Aunt "Titter" was still a kid, she accompanied her aunt on a visit to New York. They had lunch at the old, original Russian Tea Room and were served "Mushrooms Romanov." It's where she got the idea for what later became a family favorite at Thanksgiving and Christmas. You probably will like it anytime.

"Mushrooms & Sour Cream"

or "Mushrooms Romanov" if you want to be fancy. A great condiment for 4-6 people

The tools:

- 2-quart Saucepot with a lid
- Cutting board
- Cook's knife
- Big spoon

Here's what you need from the store:

- Unsalted butter
- Flour
- 1 container of sour cream
- 2 jars button mushrooms
- 1 medium sized onion
- Salt & pepper

Here's how you put it together:

1. Chop the onion.
2. Melt butter in a saucepan on medium heat.
3. Add the onion to the butter and keep heat on medium.
4. When onions look translucent, add a tablespoon of flour and stir.
5. Add the drained mushrooms.
6. Add some salt & pepper.
7. Allow this to cook for 5 minutes, stirring frequently.
8. Add the sour cream, turn the heat to low and allow to simmer on low heat for about 20 minutes, stirring every 4 or 5 minutes..

Mushrooms & Sour Cream (a.k.a. Mushrooms Romanov), reportedly, is a Ukranian specialty. The people who started The Russian Tea Room in 1927, were members of the Russian Imperial Ballet, expatriates from the ravages and misery of communism.

It is no longer on the menu, where New York's intellectual and artistic glitterati, from the late 20s once congregated to poke fun at the bourgeoise.

Mushrooms & Sour Cream is very good with steak and can be a wonderful accompaniment to roast leg of lamb. I can't recommend it with seafood but it certainly enhances meat. It's also good with almost any wine you serve, red or white.

There is nothing easier to make in these pages and I will go on record stating that if you make this for your guests, they will think you have become a culinary genius!

PRIME RIB MENU
with Crab Louis*, Mushrooms & Sour Cream & Green Beans Bearnaise

As of this writing, a standing rib roast in my store near home sells for around twelve bucks a pound. For six people including you, figure on roasting a 4-rib, bone-in piece.

1. Dry rub the roast with salt & pepper (Lawry's is best) and let stand at room temperature for about an hour and a half. Calculate the oven time at 20 minutes per pound for juicy, medium rare. Preheat the oven to 325 degrees then mount the meat on a rack (or anything which elevates it off the bottom of the pan) and put the roast in. Pay attention to the clock because you don't want to screw this up with too much oven time.

2. If you can add a little water to the bottom of the roaster without wetting the meat it will keep the drippings from blackening and they will be delicious for making gravy.

3. Once you have the roast in the oven, you and your guests can chill with a round of drinks. (4.25 lb = 1 hour, 25 min. Allow to stand 15 minutes after removing from the oven before carving.)

I have done this by enlisting two guests each to make the three other features. If people are willing, this can be a neat experience for all involved and a lot of fun.

You already have the plan for the bearnaise (from Chicken Rochambeau, page 44). The green beans need only about 20 minutes to steam (or, if you like them crunchy, you can stir-fry them in a hot skillet with some butter and olive oil for a few minutes). Ladle the bearnaise over the beans on the plates and spoon a little of it over onto the rib roast.

(The plan for the Crab Louis is on page 138).

You can't touch this at Delmonico's

This meal for six will set you back less that $100 as of this writing. A hamburger and a couple of martinis just for one will cost more than that at almost any three-star place in New York, including Delmonicos and the re-opened Russian Tea Room, where an ounce of Iranian Osetra caviar will separate you from $295.

Moreover, by the time you read this you might have to smuggle your own salt into the restaurant. At your house and in your own kitchen you can have as much fun as you can going out to eat. And your guests will definately have the same amount of fun because they *are* going out to eat.

A sandwich for when you don't have a date

Bermuda onions come from Texas today. The original growers in Bermuda got their thunder (and their market share) stolen by shrewd Texas farmers who became expert in onion culture many years ago.

The Bermuda onion is notable for its rich, sweet flavor and if you get an authentic one at the right time in the spring of the year you can slice it about a quarter-inch thick, put the slice on a piece of bread with a little mayonnaise, some salt and black pepper, then top it with another piece of mayo-ed bread and eat it just like that. Nowadays, you would probably use an authentic Vidalia onion.

Either way, it's a real good sandwich with a cold glass of Heinekin.

I know you think anybody would have to be nuts to eat that but I got the tip from no a no less respected gourmand than Ernest Hemingway, from his book *Islands in the Stream.*

The only difference was that Hemingway used peanut butter instead of the mayonnaise. Equally revolting, but probably just as good.

One day it occurred to me to make one of these to see if Hemingway was onto something or merely showing off. I had a few fresh, appropriately flat, Bermuda onions and peeled one and sliced it and made that very sandwich. It has since become a treat every now and then, especially during "Heinekin season" in the early summer.

Bermuda by way of U-boat

During World War II, some of those onions went to the bottom of the Gulf of Mexico inside the ship that was carrying them to Cuba; the tiny, 16-ton fishing/cargo vessel "Gertrude."

The "Gertrude" was sunk by the German submarine, U-166 on the night of July 16, 1942, about 40 miles northwest of Havana. Too ridiculously small to waste a torpedo on, the U-boat captain ordered the vessel destroyed by the surface cannon. Before sinking it, the captain allowed the three-man crew of "Gertrude" to get into rafts at which time he told them, using perfect English, which direction they should go to reach land.

He also asked for the name of their boat and when he heard it, he may have smiled just a bit because Gertrude was the name of his wife back in Germany.

The story of this incident, as then reported in the New York Times, included the mis-information that the Germans had stopped the boat because the crew were "desperate for provisions," without revealing that the entire cargo which went to the bottom that night was a 20-ton load of Texas onions.

There are stories about German U-boats operating in the Gulf of Mexico but precious little hard information unless you go digging for it. As kids, we were fascinated by the stories.

Some of them told of U-boat crews wearing captured Swedish naval uniforms, taking rafts up the Mississippi River channel all the way to New Orleans for a night on the town. Or of going grocery shopping and hauling back stuff for the U-Boat. Such tales are unlikely but they make good listening anyway.

There is one particular story about a U-boat sunk in the Gulf or the Caribbean which leaves behind an oil slick and debris, including bread wrappers from bakeries in Gulfport or Pass Christian, Mississippi. Yet another has a shrimp boat captain going out to meet U-boats late at night and exchanging food and supplies for money or, in some cases, gold ingots.

The reason such yarns have lasting appeal is because the very real events surrounding the very real U-boats in the Gulf were deliberately kept quiet or even officially confidential to avoid alarming an already skittish public.

But they were out there. And so were the shrimp boats and the more you don't say a thing the more that fantasy can fill the gap. The wartime press did the government's bidding on such matters.

The odd case of U-166

By the beginning of May, 1942, U-boats were sinking a lot of tonnage and killing people in the Gulf of Mexico. During that month, the Germans sank 25 ships out there. That summer, they destroyed a combined total of 33 additional ships, plying the waters along with the shrimpers.

The Kriegsmarine, or German navy, referred to 1942 as their "happy time" owing to their numerous successes. Sadly, for the U-166, it was sunk off the Louisiana coast in July, 1942, weeks after destroying the hapless "Gertrude." It met its fate almost immediately after sinking the American passenger-freighter, Robert E. Lee, by its Coast Guard escort ship.

The captain of U-166 was 27-year-old Hans Guenther Kuhlmann, pictured here with his wife, Gertrude, and with some of the officers under his command. The pictures were packed away after the war by Gertrude Kuhlmann and given to the American non-profit PAST Foundation, working with the World War II Museum in New Orleans, to feature this forgotten bit of history. You wonder what those young guys might have been able to accomplish had they not been governed by madmen and sent to the bottom of the Gulf of Mexico along with the innocent Americans they killed on board the Robert E. Lee.

KUHLMANN AND WIFE GERTRUDE

KUHLMANN AND OFFICERS

During the war, 24 U-boats cruised the Gulf, targeting oil tankers from Texas and Louisiana. They sank 56 ships. The U-166 lies today in 5,000 feet of water, less than a mile from their unfortunate victim, the Robert E. Lee, pictured here thanks to the Maritime and Seafood Industry Museum at Biloxi, Mississippi.

The World War II Museum was founded by the late historian, Stephen Ambrose in New Orleans because that is where the "Higgins" landing craft were invented and produced. These were the craft which carried thousands of soldiers and Marines ashore under fire in various invasions around the world. General Dwight Eisenhower, Supreme Allied Commander, once said that the Higgins craft "won the war for us."

ILL-FATED PASSENGER/FREIGHTER ROBERT E. LEE

What? No Chicken Marengo?

The American men and women who served at or near the front lines in all theaters of World War II were fed rations that provided nutrition but little else. The food came up to the front in crates containing cans of C-rations ("C" for combat) or K-rations; boxed, concentrated foods, developed initially for paratroops. GIs in the Pacific ate a lot of Spam (which needed no refrigeration). Redundancy bred much contempt among the troops who had to eat this food for long stretches at a time. It would serve us well to remember this the next time we sit down to enjoy a nice Porterhouse steak with sour cream and mushrooms.

"Lest We Forget - The World War II Museum"

I highly recommend that you go to New Orleans and visit this awe-inspiring place to vividly see and feel for yourself how the Second World War preserved our freedom and why freedom is anything but free. The Museum is located at 945 Magazine Street. You can check out their website at http://nationalww2museum.org.

SIMPLE ONION TART

Serves 4 as a main brunch or luncheon dish or 8 as an accompaniment

The tools:

- Cutting board
- Cook's knife
- Skillet
- 2-quart bowl

Here's what you need from the store:

- 4 or 5 onions (Bermudas can be substituted for by Vidalias)
- Olive oil
- Unsalted butter
- Fresh thyme
- 1 pint light cream
- Eggs
- Nutmeg
- Chicken base paste
- Black pepper
- One 9-inch frozen pie shell

Here's how you put it together:

1. Preheat oven to 350 degrees.

2. Slice (don't chop) 4 tennis ball-sized onions.

3. Place the slices into a skillet with some olive oil and turn the heat to medium-low.

4. Add a quarter-stick of butter.

5. Allow the onions to caramelize and turn a golden brown. This takes about 18 to 20 minutes. Stir occasionally.

5. Remove the onions to a 2-quart bowl.

6. Add a tablespoon of chicken base paste and blend it in.

7. Allow to cool slightly, about 6 minutes.

8. Add 5 extra large eggs, stir them into the onions.

9. Add one and a half mugsful of the light cream

10. Add a large spoonful of finely chopped thyme.

11. Add a half teaspoon of nutmeg.

12. Pour the mixture into a pie shell and bake at 350 for 30 minutes or when the custard "jiggles" when gently thumped.

SOME SOUTHERN COMFORTS

The Northern part of the country got over its Cajun craze a few years ago and may even be over the Southern craze by now. That is the notion that all southern food is "soul food" despite the contradiction of putting sugar in the cornbread and however wretchedly they murder the grits. If you really want good Southern cooking, just head south and eat.

That whole part of the country; roughly from Texas to the Carolinas and from North Florida to Tennessee, is blessed with wonderful food and finding it is not hard once you are a few blocks away from "interstate world" with its 9-pound, industrial grade hamburgers in "Texas-style" restaurants, with the wait staff singing "happy birthday" to embarrassed customers, all the while line dancing in cowboy boots and plaid shirts.

In the South, Southern is where you find it

Despite the amusingly facile assumptions of media commentators and the movies, the South is not a contiguous region culturally. The states can be as wildly different from one another as French-speaking Louisiana, Hillbilly Tennessee and aristocratic Natchez.

All the regions of the South are blessed with great food and finding it is not difficult. Good cooks are everywhere and a lot of them work in eating places that don't cook "soul food" or serve catfish or barbecue.

The coastal plantation elegance of Charleston lives on today in the food you find on the tables there and in New Orleans. Top-notch Creole cookery can stand proudly alongside the finest French cuisine.

My aunt, Titter, was not a professional cook but she taught me a lot about cooking over the years. Given a couple of eggs, she could turn mere squash, cheese and onions into something that would grace a menu anywhere. Hers was an inspired talent.

She lived alone for about the last 12 years of her life. I would run over there whenever I was back in town and would bring along a couple of steaks and a bottle of bourbon.

We'd solve issues of the day over drinks on the front porch. Then, as sunset waned into dusk, we'd go into the kitchen and I'd sit in the old, rickety chair that I sat in as a kid while watching her make my breakfast.

Titter would keep the discussion lively while she put the rice on and stuck a squash casserole and some yeast rolls in the oven and made the iced tea, all the while planning the outcome of a couple of thick T-bones.

Titter's Squash & Eggplant

Serves 8

The tools:

- Pot for boiling
- Cutting board
- Cook's knife
- Skillet
- 2-quart bowl
- Tablespoon
- 9 x 13" baking dish
- Coffee mug/cup

Here's what you need from the store:

- 1 medium sized onion
- 1 eggplant
- 2 medium sized yellow squash
- 1 large jalapeno
- Fine, unseasoned bread crumbs
- Eggs and butter
- Chicken base paste
- Grated Romano cheese (you will need a cup and a quarter)

Here's how you put it together:

1. Cut up the squash and peeled eggplant and put into a pot with just enough water to cover. Cover the pot and bring to a boil.

2. After 10 minutes, remove, drain and put the squash and eggplant into the bowl.

3. Chop 1 onion & 1 seeded jalapeno and fry in a skillet on medium for 4 minutes in a little unsalted butter.

4. Add this to the bowl.

5. Add a half-stick of butter to the bowl.

6. Add a cup of the Romano cheese.

7. Add three-quarters cup of bread crumbs.

8. Add 3 or 4 large or jumbo eggs.

9. Add a mounded spoonful of chicken base and as much black pepper as you want.

10. Pour this mixture into the baking dish and sprinkle the remainder of the cheese across the top. Garnish with paprika. Bake at 350 degrees for 45 minutes.

STUFFED YELLOW SQUASH

The tools:

- Pot for boiling
- Cutting board
- Cook's knife
- Skillet
- 2-quart bowl
- Tablespoon
- Baking dish
- Coffee mug

Here's what you need from the store:

- 1 medium sized sweet onion
- 1 lb. Bulk (patty) sausage
- Fine, seasoned bread crumbs
- 3 yellow squash (about 6 or 7 inches in length)
- Parmesan, Romano, and cheddar cheese

Here's how you put it together:

1. Preheat oven to 350 degrees.

2. Put the whole squash into a pot of boiling water to boil gently for 9 minutes.

3. While the squash is cooking, fry a pound of sausage (crumbled). Then drain and remove from the heat,

4. Chop the onion (fine) and fry it in the same skillet.

5. Remove the squash and let them cool.

6. In a bowl, mix the sausage and onions with a mug each of Parmesan cheese and bread crumbs.

7. Slice the squash in half lengthwise and scoop out the stuff in the middle and mix it with the stuff in the bowl.

8. Mound this mixture into the cavities, top with more Parmesan cheese and some cheddar and bake for 18 minutes.

EASY BAKED CHICKEN

The tools:

- Self draining baking pan or a bottom rack for a baking pan
- Barbecue fork or tongs
- Serving platter

Here's what you need from the store:

- Small to medium frying chicken or small roasting chicken
- Lawry's Seasoned Salt
- Black pepper

Here's how you put it together:

1. Preheat oven to 350 degrees
2. Trim the big globs of fat off the rear of the chicken (near the opening).
3. Rinse inside and out with cold water and dry with paper towels inside and out.
4. Rub seasoned salt and black pepper all over the inside and the outside.
5. Put about a 3/4 glass of water in the bottom part of your roasting pan (not touching the chicken).
6. Lay the chicken on the top portion and put it into the oven.
7. Bake for 55 minutes or until the drumstick feels ready to separate easily.
8. Turn the oven off and allow the chicken to remain inside for another 5 minutes.
9. Remove to a platter and separate and/or carve.

Baked chicken is great with the squash. The only way to screw it up is to try making it fancy. It will even create its own "au jus" if you use a double-bottom (self-draining) baking pan. It's worth it to go to the store and get one of these.

Buy a small, whole fryer instead of a "roasting chicken." It takes less time, costs less money and, in the opinion of many, tastes better than a bigger bird.

Roasted chicken is always elegant, appropriate and easy. It pairs well with just about anything. It is very good with "Mushroom & Sour Cream" (page 89), "Sweet Potatoes Thomas Jefferson" (page 10) and steamed broccoli with Bearnaise Sauce (page 45).

EASY CHICKEN MARSALA

At the store you can find thin-sliced chicken breasts, five or six slices per package. These are excellent and ready to cook with a little pounding flat to a quarter-inch thickness to tenderize them.

Season and shake in flour then gently brown in some butter over medium heat.

Remove the slices to a plate. Deglaze the hot skillet with marsala wine and/or sherry. Add a half-spoonful of chicken base and a little more marsala. Add some black pepper. Then cook the mushroom slices and some chopped green onions in that. This forms a thin sauce. Then add the meat back in and coat well. (If you want it thicker, add a small amount of flour mixed with a tablespoon or two of water). Here's another plan for these slices, utilizing fresh basil:

CREAM POACHED CHICKEN

The tools:
- Cutting board
- Cook's knife
- Cup
- Skillet
- Whisk

Here's what you need from the store:
- 1 package fresh basil
- 1 package of 5 or 6 thin-sliced chicken breasts
- Butter
- Chicken base paste
- Flour
- Half & half
- Grated Parmesan cheese
- Salt & black pepper
- Cayenne or red pepper flakes if desired

Here's how you put it together:

1. Season the thin chicken slices with salt & black pepper.
2. Put a quarter-stick of butter in the skillet on medium.
3. When the butter gets bubbly, whisk in a spoonful of flour and a spoonful of chicken base.
4. Slowly add a pint of half & half while gently whisking.
5. Rough-chop a small handful of basil leaves and add them.
6. Submerge the chicken slices in the   skillet.
7. Add cayenne and allow the slices to poach for 15 minutes.
8. Serve over steaming mounds of rice, and garnish with some whole basil leaves.

ROME: SPANISH STEPS (TRINITA DEI MONTI)
WWW.PHOTOROMA.COM

Pastafication

FRESH SEAFOOD

Three good reasons for enjoying your own pasta are that it's easy, it's virtually foolproof and it requires little if any measuring. This also applies to a seafood pasta but it is important to get the freshest possible seafood ingredients.

"Okay, sir, you gonna buy some fish today?" asked the accented little lady behind the counter.

"These scallops any good."

"Sir, I tell you, these scallops right here they the sweetest scallops you gonna' get anywhere in the ocean"

"Shrimp looks pretty good, too."

"They the best. Right off'a da boat."

"And how about the grouper? Fresh?"

"Oh my goodness, they swim into here from the sea only minutes ago."

"No kidding?"

"They family are still cryin' they miss them so."

"Really?"

"Can't you hear the mourning, the sadness? They taken from they loved ones to come into here. Tomorrow we get the loved ones, too."

"How many of the sea scallops to the pound?

"About seex, seven."

"You sure they're good?"

"You look close, you see the flavor just seepin' out."

I ordered a pound of the almost still swimming shrimp and a half-pound of the flavor-seeping scallops and a small grouper before it could escape and jump back into the ocean.

My advisor withdrew in a rustle of white butcher paper and began wrapping my order. When she had taped the items and labeled them with pricing, I thanked her for her helpfulness.

"Yes sir," she said with a sort of for-the-camera wink, "it is my pleasure to serve you."

Back home we discovered that along with her wink, she had added a little "lagniappe" to the butcher paper in the form of extra shrimp and scallops.

This melange of fresh fish and shellfish makes a light but nonetheless rich topping for spaghetti (or linguine or fettucine).

Unlike the heavier red sauces containing ground meat or Italian sausage, this combination of seafoods in a vegetable and tomato sauce won't send you to the mat after supper with a feeling of being overstuffed.

We made a caesar salad to go with it and then got stuffed.

Caesar Salad

Caesar salad was not made by or for Julius Caesar. More's the pity for old Julius. However, he did lend his name to the month of July, probably while enjoying a summer salad of oil & vinegar about 1,960 years before Caesar salad existed. The original Caesar salad was made famous by Italian expatriate, Caesar Cardini, at the restaurant which bears his name, in Tijuana, Mexico, in the early 1920's. His dressing became so popular that he bottled and sold it. Subsequent imitators copied it and eventually it became famous. Cardini's dressing is still available in stores. Yours will be better!! (See page 104.)

JULIUS CAESAR,
MARBLE VERSION

SEAFOOD PASTA IN RED SAUCE

The tools:

- Cutting board
- Cook's knife
- Garlic press
- Large skillet (12-inch)
- Coffee mug/measuring cup
- Can opener

Here's what you need from the store:

- 1 pound raw shrimp
- 1/2 pound raw scallops
- 1 pound grouper filet*
- 1 large onion (softball size)
- Celery
- Green onions
- 3 Jalapeno chiles
- Garlic
- Olive oil
- Parsley
- Grated Romano cheese
- 1 #10 can diced tomatoes
- 1 small can tomato paste
- Chicken base paste
- Fresh basil
- Dried Greek oregano
- Bay leaves
- 2 pounds spaghetti noodles (or your choice of noodle)

(any firm flesh fish will work)

Here's how you put it together:

1. Smash 3 cloves of garlic and chop the onion, 4 stalks celery, 1 bunch green onions, half-bunch fresh parsley and 3 seeded jalapeno chiles.

2. Dump these vegetables into the big skillet with about a quarter-mug of olive oil and cook on medium heat until tender (about 5 or 6 minutes).

3. Add one heaping tablespoon of chicken base.

4. the can of diced tomatoes, a half can of tomato paste, a small handful of dried Greek oregano, 4 whole bay leaves and about a quart of water.

5. Allow this to simmer on medium heat for about 45 minutes, stirring every few minutes. It will thicken as it cooks down.

6. Cut up the fish filet and add it along with the scallops and shrimp. Allow this to cook for 10 minutes.

7. Add a half-mug of finely grated Romano cheese and a handful of chopped fresh basil.

8. Allow this to simmer for another 5 minutes then serve over buttered, al dente, noodles of your choice.

CAESAR SALAD

The tools:
- Cutting board
- Skillet
- Cook's knife
- Garlic press
- Small bowl
- Big salad bowl
- Whisk

Here's what you need from the store:
- 2 heads romaine lettuce
- Anchovies or anchovy paste
- Olive oil
- Eggs
- Fresh basil
- Garlic
- Grated Parmesan cheese or Romano cheese
- Dry Coleman's English mustard
- Dried Greek oregano
- Salt & black pepper
- 1 Lemon

Your ingredients should number twelve.

Here's how you put it together:

1. Drop two eggs into butter in a skillet on medium for 14 seconds then put them in the bottom of a big salad bowl. Whisk briskly.

2. Add a small handful finely chopped fresh basil.

3. Add about a spoonful of dried oregano.

4. Add a spoonful of anchovy paste.

5. Add about a quarter cup of olive oil.

6. Add 1 large clove of garlic, smashed.

7. Add a handful of parmesan cheese.

8. Add a spoonful of coleman's English dry mustard.

9. Add the juice of a half lemon. Whisk all this briskly.

10. Add the cleaned, chopped and dry romaine. Toss until it's all nicely coated.

11. *OPTIONAL:* for a one-dish meal, lay on some tender strips of broiled chicken breasts or a handful of cooked and seasoned shrimp).

Credit for this truly great Caesar salad goes to my friend, Jim Evans, who patiently walked me through the first one I ever made. Jim served with the old U.S. Army Air Corps in Italy during World War II and nowadays runs a small winery on his property near the picturesque town of Oley, Pennsylvania. (Photo: John Rider)

"Joy of the mountains"

Now, a word about using dried Greek oregano since it is called for it all the time. If you have a specialty Mediterranean store nearby or if you see one in your travels, stop and buy a bag.

An informed source who is Greek and also a good friend told me that the best oregano is grown on the mountain slopes of Greece and that the name "oregano" is Greek and translates to "oros" or mountain and "ganos" or joy; i.e "joy of the mountains."

You'll find this oregano still on the stems of the original plant and you crush one section of the package, cut a small hole in the end corner and shake the loose oregano out onto a small plate. That way you can remove any little twigs that might be included with the dried leaves. Then just put the bag into a ziplock for storage. I thank my brother, Alex Cotten for the tip.

Basic red meat sauce for spaghetti

You can make this with any ground meat. However, if you're bored with the usual ground beef in this sauce, you might try a 50/50 blend of ground chicken and ground pork. Why? Well, because ground beef is a little heavy and the pork and chicken add a measure of sweetness. You can toss in some cut up Italian sausage, smoked sausage or kielbassa if you want to but I don't recommend andouille because of the strong flavors it imparts.

There are competing claims for the origin of spaghetti, ranging from the Chinese to the Sicilians, the latter allegedly inheriting it from Marco Polo who might have brought it back from China. Some apparently still maintain that the Chinese invented pasta noodles but, with apologies to the Chinese, that just doesn't seem to work. 100-year old eggs, yes. Spaghetti, no.

It may be that the U.S. Supreme Court will someday have to rule on the origin of spaghetti. If they can declare a fruit such as the tomato legally to be a vegetable, then they ought to just state outright, in an actual law, that spaghetti was invented by the Italians and get it over with.

Besides, the Chinese already have mushu pork, wonton soup, stinky tofu and moogoo gai pan. What more do they need?

BASIC RED SAUCE FOR SPAGHETTI

The tools:
- Pot for boiling
- Colander
- Cutting board
- Cook's knife
- 1 large & medium skillet
- 2-quart bowl
- Tablespoon & teaspoon
- Coffee mug
- Can opener
- Bowl

Here's what you need from the store:
- 1 softball-sized onion
- Green onions
- Celery
- Parsley
- Garlic
- Jalapeno chiles
- 1 pound ground pork
- 1 pound ground chicken
- 1 #10 can diced tomatoes
- 1 small can tomato paste
- Dried oregano
- Gravy Master
- Chicken base paste
- Fresh basil/ dried bay leaves
- Olive oil
- Black pepper
- Finely grated Pecorino Romano cheese

Here's how you put it together:

1. Chop 1 onion, 4 stalks of celery, 1 bunch of green onions, a quarter-bunch of fresh parsley, 3 seeded jalapeno chiles and smash 3 cloves of garlic and put this in the bowl.

2. Pour some olive oil into the large skillet with the heat on medium.

3. Add the chopped vegetables.

4. In a separate skillet, add the ground meats and turn the heat to high. Allow meats to brown (about 8 minutes) while occasionally stirring.

5. When the meats have browned, add them to the vegetables in the large skillet.

6. Add 2 tablespoons chicken base paste.

7. Add the can of diced tomatoes.

8. Add a half can of tomato paste.

9. Add a small handful of the dried oregano.

10. Add a big handful of chopped fresh basil.

11. Add a teaspoon of gravy master and 3 or 4 bay leaves.

12. Add black pepper to taste.

13. Allow this to gently simmer uncovered for about one hour.

14. Add a big handful of finely grated Romano cheese and stir in well. Let this simmer on medium low until it gets to the right thickness.

GET YOUR STUFF TOGETHER IN ONE PLACE . . .

. . . FOR MAKING RED SAUCE!

"When in Rome"

Regardless of whether the Italians invented pasta it's correct to say they did. Besides, it might even be a legal finding someday.

Like Cajun food, the great flavors of Italian food are derived from basic stuff, typically without a lot of add-ons or fine tuning ("a pinch" of anything, etc.) or heavy, cream-or-alcohol-rich sauces.

Italians had to invent pasta because it reflects their unique approach to the enjoyment of every kind of good food, which is to say it reflects the Italians themselves, which is to say it reflects people who really like to eat.

Pretend that you are homesick in Rome one night, wandering around looking for supper. The city's politicians have ordered all street lights to be turned off at dusk, so this expedition becomes interesting as you try to locate curbsides and escape death from tiny automobiles by crossing the street. The cars amaze you because they all appear to be going eighty miles an hour through the darkened streets, apparently hoping to kill pedestrians dumb enough to step off the sidewalk. At last, famished, you stumble down a narrow canyon of a street and into a small, family run trattoria.

"Could you repeat that in English, Signore Hoss?"

Mounted in the rear corner of this little place is a black-and-white television. It is running an old "Bonanza" episode. There is Hoss Cartwright in his multi-gallon hat, overdubbed in an odd, twangy, Italian. Little Joe, speaking overdubbed Italian from the saddle of his horse, alternates lines with old Ben Cartwright, babbling away in a high-pitched Italian voice that reminds you of what Enrico Caruso might have sounded like had tried to recite Tennessee Williams.

You don't speak Italian but that's okay because it's obvious that you are an American and that they could over-dub you anytime they felt like it and, besides, you might be one of the Cartwright relatives, having left the Ponderosa to come all this way just to have supper in their cozy little eatery on the Via Mario de Fiori.

So, even if you aren't at home, it is kind of like home and your homesickness backs off just a bit. Moreover, you get this huge plate of spaghetti and a rich, tomato and eggplant sauce, topped with a big handful of grated Parmesan and served with fresh, homemade bread.

Somehow, in that big, dark, city you start feeling familiar things.

You leave happy, with the several-times repeated blessings of the family and a full belly and make your way back to the hotel by a sort of dead reckoning, although you don't like to use the word "dead" in any context. Every few minutes another tiny car smokes its way past you in a deafening whine.

Then a strange thing happens:

"Ain't no sun up in the sky . . ."

In pitch darkness somebody is whistling Harold Arlen's unforgettable "Stormy Weather" and you have to stop and listen. Whoever the whistler is knows all the notes and shapes them just right. That quintessentially American tune seems to resonate from all directions in the black of night, lending the unexpected comfort of a suddenly appearing, familiar old friend, no less than the stars visible above Rome now that the lights have been turned off; Cassiopeia hovers above a darkened office building, the great Square of Pegasus is directly overhead: The same stars you would see from your own backyard every fall remind you that you still have your own backyard waiting for you.

> **Harold Arlen**
> 02/15/05 - 04/23/86
> *"Come Rain or Come Shine"*
> *"Over the Rainbow"*
> *"Let's Fall in Love"*
> *"I've Got the World on a String"*
> *"That Old Black Magic"*
> *"One for My Baby"*
> *"Between the Devil & the Deep Blue Sea"*
> *"Stormy Weather*

WE GET THE FETTUCCINE PART BUT WHO WAS ALFREDO?

Maybe by now you can actually order "Fettuccine Alfredo" anywhere in Italy and expect the waiter to know what you're talking about.

The reason is there is no single recipe for this in the country. There is no single recipe for it anywhere else, either.

The fame of serving fettuccine noodles on a plate with a lot of butter and cream and Parmesan cheese started in 1914, when Alfredo DeLilio served it to his sickly wife to jump-start her appetite. It worked. She got hungry.

But what it really started was Alfredo's restaurant career, when he began making a big show of his fettuccine at tableside after opening his own place in Rome; "Alfredo alla Scrofa."

Alfredo would wheel the steaming noodles and butter and Parmesan cheese to your table and with flourish mix the components and tong them onto your plate.

He became a food entertainer. He called himself "the emperor of the fettuccine" and he turned into something of a legend, including among his patrons the famous newlywed movie stars, Douglas Fairbanks and Mary Pickford.

So impressed were they by Alfredo that they gave him a gold spoon and fork, recently received as a wedding gift, which he incorporated into his act and which became a lasting part of the restaurant's logo. The restaurant was handed off to his son, Alfredo, Jr. who continued his father's tableside showmanship as well as the practice of hanging the walls with pictures of illuminati, among them John Wayne, Alfred Hitchcock, Ella Fitzgerald and Elizabeth Taylor.

You realize, of course, that the food puritans and their inquisitors probably consider serving Fettuccine Alfredo a crime and that their lawyers will someday get it designated as attempted second degree manslaughter if you serve it to your guests and as attempted suicide if you just sit in a room and eat it all by yourself.

I wish that I could be the geneticist who one day makes the inevitable discovery that there is a human "mess-with" gene because it would provide the scientific basis for my hypothesis that humans are biologically hard-wired to annoy the living hell out of each other just for the sheer, pleasure of it.

Helmut Schoeck's book on envy, which bears the same title, demonstrated through brilliant research that people do, in fact, take pleasure in knowing that anyone whom they perceive to be better than they are in any way are brought low and made to suffer. This, he maintains, is the psychology behind most so called "blue laws," banning people from one sort of enjoyment or another. Such laws create black markets wherever they turn up – as in Prohibition or the tax code.

FETTUCCINE ALFREDO

FETTUCCINE ALFREDO

The tools:

- Pot for boiling
- Colander
- Large skillet
- Whisk
- Big serving fork or pasta server
- Tablespoon
- Coffee mug/measuring cup

Here's what you need from the store:

- 1-pound package Barilla or de Cecco fettuccine noodles
- Light cream or half & half
- Lemon
- Nutmeg
- Unsalted Butter
- Grated parmesan cheese (you need about a pound)
- White pepper (or black)

Here's how you put it together:

1. Bring 5 or 6 quarts of water to a boil and add a half-cup of salt.
2. Add the fettuccine noodles and cook until "al dente."
3. Drain the noodles in the colander.
4. Heat a pint of the cream in a large skillet.
5. Add the juice of one lemon and blend with a whisk.
6. Add a stick of the unsalted butter and slowly whisk over medium heat until the butter melts, about a 2 or 3 minutes.
7. Add the cooked fettuccine noodles and toss thoroughly.
8. Add one and three-quarters cups of grated Parmesan cheese and blend.
9. Add the remaining half-pint of cream and blend.
10. Add a sprinkle of nutmeg and some white pepper then blend and stir for about a minute before serving.

Alfredo "Sauce"

Simply combine a pint of cream or half & half with a stick of butter, a big handful of Parmesan cheese a spoonful of chicken base (don't use salt) and some black or white pepper over medium heat. Leave out the lemon juice and the nutmeg. Thin with milk if necessary.

"Salsa Alfredo con salsa di pomodoro"

I don't know if this really means "Alfredo sauce with tomato sauce" but it sounds more upscale than pig Latin.

Translations can be tricky, especially if you try to make them using common sense. We had a booth at a big food show in Paris one year, trying to sell the pies my company made to the rest of the world. Before going over there, we spent a great deal of time (and not a little bit of money) printing our brochures in French.

One of the things we wanted to translate was "no preservatives" because we made a point of always saying that. However, our American translator put that French phrase in as "sans preservatifs," which you may be relieved to discover means "no condoms" in French.

"SANS PRESERVATIFS"

So we went to all that trouble and expense just to let everybody in the world know that our pies contained no condoms, which must have been welcome news indeed.

I wondered why all those people at the booth were chuckling to themselves as they read our homemade "French language" brochure.

Anyway, you can blend a very simple tomato sauce with the very simple Alfredo sauce and come up with something that is different from either one but just as good in its own right, especially if you throw in slices of chicken or fried mushrooms or shrimp.

You can make the tomato sauce ahead of time, keep it in the refrigerator up to four days (or just freeze it for whenever) and then heat it and blend it with the Alfredo sauce whenever you get the Alfredo sauce made.

There is nothing really complicated about the tomato sauce. You just make the basic meat sauce for spaghetti but leave out the meat (see page 106).

It's a good idea whenever you make a basic tomato sauce to make enough of it to freeze for a later application. A good way to do this is to pour your (cooled) sauce into a ziplock freezer bag, smash out as much of the air as you can and then seal it. This will prevent the freezer temperatures from pulling moisture out of the sauce and making "frost" out of it which can compromise the flavor. This typically is what happens if you try to store and freeze your sauce in a rigid container.

THE ROAD TO NAPLES

In Rome, a few years ago, the UN sponsored the World Food Conference. We were there, doing a documentary film.

Although its primary purpose was to make you feel scared that the world was going to end soon and to make you feel guilty for being the main cause of it, you could actually come away with a better understanding of why there were so many hungry people in the poorest parts of the world.

Here's one of the more compelling reasons:

Every day, the dignitaries dozed through agonizing reports of kids starving in those poor countries. They were especially hungry in those destitute, ex-colonial nations where the limousined, military-garbed and ribbon-festooned rulers were fat and had even fatter Swiss bank accounts and villas at Antibes or Cannes and had cargo ships lined up at their state-of-the-art docks, stuffed to the gunn'ls with AK-47s and surface-to-air missiles and cognac and whole, shrink-wrapped pallets of cash and Rolexes to give to visiting movie stars as favors. To resolve this untenable situation, the world's esteemed dignitaries at Rome proposed (need I tell you) sending more cash.

Just a day or so past a week of this, when we all suspected we may be going nuts, my producer, Bill Norris and cameraman, Spurgeon May and I decided to run down to Naples to film something important, although now I can't remember what it was.

More than likely, we just opted for a day on the lam to escape the bitter irony of those "shame on us" diatribes and the antacid-inducing lunches at the Mussolini-built Palazzo dei Congressi and have an opportunity to escape the incessant car horns of Rome.

You may not be aware of this but the horn is the most important part of a car in Rome. It is the most used part. Brakes seem to be optional. In Rome, you get the impression that traffic lights are suggestions and that the main reason for building intersections is so Romans have a space for getting out of their cars and punching each other in the nose.

It's almost like driving in Boston.

Our driver, Fulvio, picked us up at the hotel and we headed south, filming along the way. Whenever a place looked interesting, we'd get Fulvio to stop and Spurgeon would jump out, grab his gear from the trunk, and shoot some film.

As we rolled onto the wharf at Anzio, a fishing trawler was just then chugging out to sea. It was a beautiful image, with crewmen readying nets and lines and a thin trail of engine smoke wafting behind them. I asked Spurgeon to get some footage of it. Suddenly, in the middle of a long, graceful pan we were surrounded by police cars with flashing blue lights and placed under arrest by officers of the Captain of the Port. We were criminals, guilty of having no permit to take pictures!

They took us to headquarters where we were interrogated by a body double of Caesar Romero, the old Hollywood actor; his uniform coat stylishly draped over his shoulders in the manner of a continental and his peaked hat reminding you of old newsreels of Juan Peron on the balcony.

By the time we were pardoned and set free, it was decided to scratch going to Naples and just have lunch and a nice drink or two at the restaurant next door.

The only people in the place besides the cooks were four waiters neatly dressed in crisp, white jackets with brass buttons and black bow ties. They apparently were happy that three Americans had wandered in there that afternoon to give them and the chef something to do.

"Here, Try this!"

Having just gone through a near-jail experience, it didn't matter that we were foils for the waiters. They were having fun. We were having fun. We were getting plastered.

Every few minutes one of the gregarious waiters would pour something into our glasses at no charge, proudly stating its name and pedigree in excited Italian which Fulvio translated.

"Okay to drink. Not okay to drink. Maybe yes, maybe no. You get sick." And so on.

Then lunch. I forget what was on my plate but it was not the frutti di mare. Fulvio had that and ate it with such gusto and relish that I determined to get it the next time I was in Anzio, maybe even before then, and also to try preparing it when I got back home.

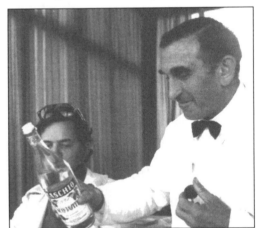

PRODUCER BILL NORRIS, ENJOYING A LITTLE EXTRACURRICULAR LIBATION FROM OUR WAITER AT THE DOCKSIDE RESTAURANTE IN ANZIO.

FRUITS OF THE SEA

Around the coastline of Italy, you can find open air fish markets set up to display the day's catch of calamari, octopus, sardines, langostina, anchovies and other varieties of fish, sorted and displayed in shallow wooden bins set up on tables. It can be amusing to watch some of the creatures with legs crawling out of their bins and across the tops of the others, apparently trying to make a run for it back to the ocean. My helpful Mexican seafood lady down in Orange Beach could make some hay with that I think.

FRUTTI DI MARE

(or Sopa di Pesche or Seafood Stew or whatever)

The tools:

- Cutting board
- Cook's knife
- Mug /cup
- Can opener
- Jigger
- Clean brush for scrubbing shellfish
- Corkscrew

Here's what you need from the store:

- Olive oil
- Garlic
- Small onion
- Green onions
- Crushed red pepper flakes
- White wine
- Raw shrimp*
- Blue crabs, cleaned and halved*
- Clams*
- Mussels*
- a firm-fleshed fish (haddock or grouper)*
- Lemon
- Bay leaves

* Frutti di Mare is all how you want to make it. These are suggested ingredients and you can add the amount that suits you best. Feel free to swap out lobster for crabs, crawfish for shrimp; add calamari, and/or any other fish/shellfish you want.

Here's how you put it together:

1. Saute 1 small chopped onion, 3 cloves of smashed garlic and some red pepper flakes in oil on medium heat. Stir constantly.

2. After 6 minutes, add a half-mug of white wine, the juice of one lemon and 2 or 3 bay leaves.

3. Add some salt (or substitute with a little lobster base paste) and allow this to simmer on medium.

4. Add the tomatoes, cut in half and the juice.

5. Add the clams and mussels and put a lid on the pan for 6 minutes.

6. Add the shrimp and the halved crabs and allow to continue cooking for about 5 minutes.

7. Add a small handful chopped parsley. Remove any shells that have not opened. Add the fish filet and chopped green onions. Remove the bay leaves. Cover and cook slowly for 8 minutes (If adding calamari [squid] do it now).

Some of the appeal of frutti di mare is that it is tactile; you get your fingers involved when you're eating it and get your friends involved when you're making it. You can leave the shells on the shrimp if you want and also toss in some shucked oysters and crab claws. You might even want to incorporate a few whole crawfish. I generally use lobster base in place of salt.

But If you're really hungry, make lasagne

One of the best reasons not to make lasagne is that you first have to boil those big, flat pieces of pasta with the curly edges and drain them etc.

Now you don't have to.

You can buy the flat pasta ready to go right out of the box and into the lasagne, no boiling necessary.

Lasagne is a lot easier if you made more than enough meat sauce beforehand and have it available in your freezer. If not, well, it's still easy. Just make the red meat sauce that you did earlier (page 106) and you'll be on your way to a good lasagne.

You should keep in mind that what you want is a sauce that isn't "bulky" with big chunks of meat and sausage and thin enough so that it spreads easily and evenly over the layers beneath it. You want the sauce to be a little "juicy."

The following is my own adaptation based loosely on several other plans. After you make lasagne a couple of times, you'll develop an idea of things that might improve it, such as using a nutmeg-seasoned bechamel sauce and different cheeses.

Try to get the lasagne out of the oven before it becomes too dry. A really good lasagne is normally a little runny.

LASAGNE

(This plan assumes that you already have the red meat sauce: page 106)

The tools:
- 9 x 14 x 3 inch non-reactive casserole dish
- Large bowl

Here's what you need from the store:
- 1 box Barilla, no-boil lasagne sheets
- 2 pound package shredded mozzarella cheese
- 1 pound package grated Parmesan or fresh Romano cheese.
- 2 pounds of ricotta cheese
- Eggs
- Nutmeg
- Paprika
- Olive oil

Here's how you put it together:

1. Blend the ricotta cheese with 4 large or extra large eggs.

2. Grease a 9 x 14 x 3 casserole dish (tomato sauce means NO aluminum!).

3. Preheat oven to 350 degrees.

4. Lay enough dry lasagne sheets in the bottom of the casserole dish to cover the bottom (okay to overlap a little).

5. Spread enough red meat sauce over this amply to cover.

6. Spread some of the parmesan cheese over this just to cover.

7. Spread some of the ricotta cheese and egg mixture over that by dropping walnut-sized globs all around and mashing slightly.

8. Spread some of the mozzarella cheese over that.

9. Lay down another layer of the lasagne sheets.

10. Repeat the layers as per above, starting with the red meat sauce and ending with mozzarella.

11. Sprinkle paprika around the edges of the mozzarella cheese top and bake at 350 degrees for 30-40 minutes until lightly browned and bubbly.

(Imported, Italian Romano is made from the milk of sheep (pecorino). The domestic variety frequently is made from cow's milk. True, Italian pecorino Romano cheese will not turn "stringy" in your sauces.)

CHICKEN LASAGNE

Different from the other lasagne but equally tasty!

The tools:
- 10 x 14 x 3 inch casserole dish
- Large bowl
- Garlic press
- Cook's knife
- Cutting board
- A couple of skillets

Here's what you need from the store:
- 1 box Barilla, no-boil lasagne sheets
- 2-pound package shredded mozzarella cheese
- 2-pound package ricotta cheese
- 1 pound package grated Parmesan or Romano
- Eggs
- 1-1/2 pounds ground chicken
- Nutmeg
- Paprika
- Olive oil
- Large onion
- Garlic
- 3 jalapeno chiles
- Green onion
- Parsley
- Fresh basil
- Fresh mushrooms (sliced)
- Chicken base paste
- 1 quart half & half
- Flour

Here's how you put it together:
1. Blend the ricotta cheese with 4 large or extra large eggs.
2. Grease a 10 x 14 x 3 casserole dish.
3. Chop the onion, a half-bunch green onions, a quarter-bunch of parsley, a small bunch of fresh basil, a clove of garlic, one package fresh mushrooms (sliced) and 3 seeded jalapenos.
4. Fry the vegetables in some olive oil until tender (fry the mushrooms separately on high heat until golden).
5. Put all the vegetables in a bowl.
6. Fry 1-1/2 pounds ground chicken.
7. In a large skillet on medium heat, blend a tablespoon of flour with 4 tablespoons olive oil.
8. Add a tablespoon of chicken base paste.
9. While whisking, slowly incorporate a quart of half & half.
10. When the sauce gets thick, add all the vegetables and the cooked ground chicken and blend to make the sauce.
11. Alternate layers: lasagne noodles, chicken-vegetable sauce, shredded mozzarella, ricotta and egg mixture and repeat.
12. Spread mozzarella across the top, sprinkle with some paprika and bake 50 minutes at 350 degrees.

Notes: _____

_____

_____

_____

_____

_____

_____

_____

_____

_____

_____

_____

_____

_____

_____

_____

_____

_____

_____

_____

_____

_____

_____

OYSTERMAN WILLIAM STEVENS
COURTESY OF NEW YORK STATE ARCHIVES

"Pass the lemon then notify the undertaker."

OYSTER TALES

One of life's enduring pleasures is to stand at a tin-sheathed bar quaffing a pitcher of beer and devouring a plate of ice cold, freshly shucked oysters. To taste the salty subtleties of this flavor-packed mollusk is to absorb the very "essence of ocean" and also to realize that life is as short as it is sweet.

But there is a slight hitch.

You should know that the Center for Science in the Public Interest, a Ralph Nader spinoff and one of the most successful promoters of food hysteria since the Third Reich, estimates that, as of this writing, 135 people have died from eating raw oysters in the United States since 1989, which is about seven deaths per year.

The oyster industry guesses that 20 million Americans eat raw oysters each year, putting your odds of death by oyster in the U.S. at 1 in 3 million. For the record, there are 48 U.S. deaths on average each year from lightning. So, run me out another dozen on the halfshell, thank you. I'll live with the odds.

The fatalities that result from eating oysters in the raw come from the bacterium, vibrio vulnificus, which can sometimes be found in warm sea water from late April to about the first week of November. This is especially true in the Gulf of Mexico, from whence many of the best tasting oysters in the country are harvested. The other harmful germ in some oysters is called vibrio parahemolyticus, which won't kill you but can make you very sick.

The skinny on those "R" months

The old rule of avoiding raw oysters in any month without an "R" in it derives in part from this seasonal phenomenon and in major part also from the absence of refrigeration in the past (although the ancient Romans packed them in snow in northern France and carried them in sacks all the way back to Rome). The vibrio bacteria have no odor or taste and do not alter the appearance of the oyster meats so there is no way to tell if an oyster is infected before you eat it.

Another reason the "non-R" months sport a red flag is because the oysters are spawning. When the water temperature gets above 73 degrees, the spawn has begun and runs typically from May through early Fall. During this time, the oysters become depleted, if not exhausted, causing them to diminish in size and firmness. It is this more than anything which makes them unappetizing. Then, when the water drops below 72 degrees in the fall, typically in November in the northern Gulf, the oysters firm up, fatten up and become nice and plump. They stay that way until the next spawn starts.

How to get fresh tasting oysters all year 'round

Since you can't keep in-shell oysters on ice for months at a time, they must be frozen for year-round consumption. Companies which pack oysters have to reduce potential bacteria in them to "non detectable levels." They do this by a process using extremely cold temperatures which flash-freeze the oysters. Such freezing occurs so rapidly that ice crystals don't form in the flesh to cause damage resulting in "mushy" meat and if any vibrio are lurking, they are gone in a flash. Amazingly, the meat stays plump and almost as fresh as just caught.

One of these companies is Leavins Seafood, on the bay in the sleepy little Florida Panhandle town of Apalachicola. This is where 90 percent of Florida's oysters come from. The Leavins Company is the biggest player in the region.

Grady Leavins (pronounced "L-evans") and his wife, Alice, started the company in 1973, having quit their day jobs as biological researchers at the University of Florida.

GRADY & ALICE LEAVINS

Today, at the annual Oyster Festival in October, Grady receives the title "King Retsyo" ("oyster" backwards). To overcome the fear of eating raw oysters, Grady got the term "Fearless Oyster" as a trademark and has used it in marketing his oysters.

I visited the Leavins plant in Apalachicola and was provided a walk-through by Grady, who showed me how the oysters were cleaned, shucked, flash-frozen and packaged in sturdy boxes that hold 12-dozen oysters each in plastic trays. The Leavins company ships these individually quick frozen (I.Q.F.) oysters to foodservice distributors who then sell to restaurants, hotels, cruise lines and others. Sadly, they don't sell retail to you and me but it's good to know that they're in many restaurants.

First encounter of the raw kind

My dad and his buddies drove from our place near West Panama City Beach to Apalachicola one morning for a sack of oysters. They got back to the beach around 1 p.m. and set up shop on the screened porch with ice, beer and a big burlap sack of oysters. We boys had been on the beach and in the water from just after breakfast and by the time we dragged ourselves out of the surf and went up for lunch we were famished. The men wanted to see if I could stomach a raw oyster, thinking that I would either decline or give it a try and throw up for their amusement.

But when you're that hungry, you accept the offer. I ate one raw, freshly shucked oyster on a cracker with some Tabasco and horseradish on it and found it surprisingly good. I asked for another.

"I ain't ever seen a kid eat one of these," said Mr. Fawcett.

"You actually like that?" asked my dad.

Mr. Whittle offered me a sip of beer which I declined, preferring a long draught of water from the garden hose. Besides the timeless joy of ice cold halfshell oysters, they're also good other ways. Here's one of those:

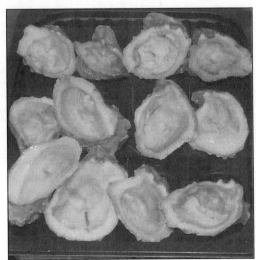

Oyster Pudding

The tools:

- Colander
- Bread knife, electric knife or any sawtooth knife
- 2-quart bowl
- 9 x 13 x 3 inch baking dish
- Whisk

Here's what you need from the store:

- 2 pints fresh raw oysters
- Plain white bread
- Unsalted butter
- 16 ounces shredded yellow cheddar cheese
- Large eggs
- 1 quart of half & half
- Salt, pepper, paprika

Here's how you put it together:

1. Preheat oven to 350 degrees.

2. Strain and pick through the oysters to remove any shell bits.

3. Spread soft butter on one side of six or more bread slices.

4. Slice the buttered bread into small cubes.

5. Layer the baking dish as follows:

    (a) buttered bread cubes,

    (b) oysters,

    (c) grated cheese,

    (Repeat the layers).

6. Mix half & half with salt & pepper and whisk this with the eggs.

7. Pour the liquid over everything to near the top. Garnish with a little more cheese and sprinkle paprika around the outside edges of the top.

8. Bake at 350 degrees for 40 minutes.

9. Allow to "set" for 10 minutes before serving.

This splendid dish tastes so good that even some people who normally don't eat oysters enjoy it. There is a particularly unmistakable flavor of the sea that oysters impart to various foods and this is definitely one of the best of them.

Be sure to get the freshest oysters possible if you are shucking them yourself or get the ones with the best reputation if you're using the already shucked variety. Any oyster meats which have started to taste gamey might still be edible but they will not be good in anything.

You may wish to reserve some of the oyster liquid to blend with the eggs and half & half but sometimes the addition of this liquid can make the dish taste too strong.

You can "dress up" the oyster pudding by mixing 3/4 cup of bread crumbs with a little melted butter and sprinkling this over the top before baking. Sadly, this dish does not freeze well and it goes downhill fast in the refrigerator. So make it and eat it!

Oyster pudding can be served as a main course or as a compliment to a main course such as a rib roast. It goes extremely well with a freshly baked ham. In fact, you can make a great impression at your table with exactly that combination.

Oyster pudding is similar to a thing variously named "scalloped oysters" or "escalloped oysters," typically using saltine crackers instead of bread cubes, frequently without the use of cheese. Both are "built" with alternating layers and then finished off by pouring the seasoned liquid portion over the top when completed.

Is this the origin of spring break?

The first evidence we have of a thriving oyster culture derives from vases uncovered at the town of Baiae, near the Bay of Naples. Scenes on the vases depict oysters being harvested from aquaculture beds that were introduced by Sergius Orata around 97 BC. Sergius was a Roman official whose dedicated love for oysters made him famous.

Baiae was a resort town where many wealthy and well-connected Romans went to debauch themselves with wine and sex and wild beach parties. It was the main source of cultivated oysters during the period and savvy entrepreneurs made a lot of money catering to the debauchees.

Around 44 BC, after Caesar had conquered Britain, Romans began importing oysters from the cold ocean waters around the British coastline. These oysters were packed in burlap bags filled with enough snow to insure that they remained alive and fresh for the journey to Italy, where many considered them to have aphrodisiac qualities.

Indeed, Aphrodite herself is famously depicted by Botticelli emerging from an oyster shell at birth. Years later, another famous Italian party animal named Casanova, reportedly ate 12 dozen oysters at a sitting to improve his appetite for sex.

Roman sites in Britain itself indicate that the Roman occupiers

BIRTH OF VENUS BY SANDRO BOTTICELLI

enjoyed the British oysters, too. Ancient Roman oyster shell piles have been found as far north in England as Hadrian's Wall. The Celts in Britain had long enjoyed their oysters prior to Roman times and with the occupation came a renewed enthusiasm for them, leading to a brisk business trade in oysters across the British Isles as well as all the way to Rome.

Origin of a Familiar Phrase

"The world is my oyster," thought to refer to the opportunity that awaits youthful ambition actually is a phrase from Shakespeare's play *Falstaff*. One of the characters, refused a loan by Falstaff, tells him: "well then, the world's mine oyster . . . I will with sword open."

This meant that he would use his sword to pry open the purses of victims anywhere in the world to get what he wanted. It didn't mean a real oyster, although it would have been fun watching him try to open one with a sword.

FRIED OYSTERS

As long as you're buying shucked oysters, you may as well go ahead and pick up an extra pint or so for breading and frying. Doing this creates a bit of a mess and you have to get your fingers sticky* but the taste is more than worth the effort and the actual production is easy.

Shake your raw oysters in a Ziplock bag with some flour mixed with a little corn meal, salt and pepper to coat.

Then fry 6 or 8 at a time in a 10-inch skillet (or bigger) with enough peanut oil (400 degrees) to float them in for 2-3 minutes. Drain on paper towels. They are incredibly delicious!

A real treat is to make or buy some good tartar sauce, lather up the insides of an oven-heated baguette with it, add sliced tomatoes and lettuce then pack the whole thing with hot, freshly fried oysters. That's the basic oyster po'boy and if you get really good bread to start with and keep practicing, you might save yourself from having to go all the way to New Orleans to get one. On second thought, it's better just to go to New Orleans.

* (If you don't like sticky fingers, go to your local restaurant supply store and get a box of disposable latex foodservice gloves. These are also good for making hand-tossed salads. The average man's hand requires size extra large).

Baking oysters in the shell

Oysters baked under a variety of toppings, from simple to extravagant, are worthy additions to your table. Here is a plan named for my barbecue loving British friends Richard and Jenny Boxall. When I was at their house in France, I attempted to make what I thought I remembered as Oysters Mosca in the shell but drew a blank. I drew a blank because we started cocktails early. You're forced to invent in such times or suffer the loss of face.* I remembered too late that Oysters Mosca is not made in the shell so I renamed it:

* Oysters Mosca is a great New Orleans dish, for years served at the Elmwood Plantation. It is not baked in the shell. Wisdom admonishes: "never start cocktails before five and then cook."

OYSTERS BOXALL

Serves 4

The tools:

- Oyster knife
- Cook's knife
- Garlic press
- Cutting board
- Baking sheet(s)
- Rock salt (optional)
- Skillet, spoon, etc.

Here's what you need from the store:

- 4 or 5 dozen nice-sized live, in-shell, oysters
- Butter
- Olive oil
- Green onions
- Parsley
- Fresh garlic
- Italian bread crumbs
- Parmesan cheese
- Pernod (of Ricard)
- Dried Greek oregano
- Lemon
- Salt, pepper, cayenne

Here's how you put it together:

1. Wash the oysters then shuck by removing the top (flatter) shell and cutting the adductor muscle underneath the oyster meat in the bottom shell.

2. Lay these on baking sheets, held steady by some rock salt or wads of aluminum foil (to hold the liquid in).

3. Very finely chop a half-bunch of green onions and 3 or 4 cloves of garlic,(or just smash it with a press) and a half bunch of parsley.

4. Fry the chopped vegetables in the butter and olive oil until they are soft.

5. Add a big handful of Parmesan cheese, two handfuls bread crumbs, a jigger of Pernod, a spoonful of crushed, dried Greek oregano, the juice of half a lemon and the salt & the peppers to taste.

6. Bake at 400 degrees for 18 minutes.,

OYSTERS ROCKEFELLER

The tools:

- Oyster knife
- Cook's knife
- Garlic press
- Cutting board
- Baking sheet
- Rock salt
- Skillet

Here's what you need from the store:

- 1 dozen live oysters
- Butter
- Bacon
- Green onions
- Fresh spinach
- Watercress
- Italian
- Parmesan cheese
- Jack cheese
- Pernod

Here's how you put it together:

1. Preheat oven to 400 degrees.

2. Place the bacon in the freezer for 20 minutes ahead of time. When it firms up, chop it very finely.

3. Put the chopped bacon in a skillet on medium heat and gently brown it.

4. Very finely chop the following and add them to the skillet: One clove garlic, one big handful mushrooms, two handfuls of spinach, a small handful green onions a small handful of parsley.

5. Add a half stick of butter, a medium handful of bread crumbs, a small handful of Parmesan cheese and a jigger of Pernod. Stir this well then remove to the refrigerator for one hour.

6. Shuck the oysters (see Oysters Boxall, page 127) and stuff them with the cold mixture, placing a small amount of the jack cheese on top of each one.

7. Bake at 400 degrees for 16 minutes.

Stuffed oysters require the cutting board because it is hard to get a good consistency for the vegetables with a processor. Get everything finely chopped. For example, the mushroom pieces should be chopped to about the size of small peas and the green onions to about the size of rice grains.

One nice thing about this plan is that you can double it, roll it up in a good wrap and keep it in the refrigerator for up to a week. Freezing it probably would cause separation.

PHOTO: FLORIDA DEPARTMENT
OF AGRICULTURE

CHOWDER DAYS

On a cold, Florida Saturday in March a few years back, David Hackney drove down to my old beach place with his canoe in the back of the truck and we set off for the salt marsh to catch clams.

It wasn't far. The marsh was 200 yards behind my house and we thought because the weather was so miserable and cold that it would be a good idea to wade in cold, muddy water, looking for clams in the slimy goo under the bottom.

Back then, you could harvest fresh oysters at low tide without a permit. You simply broke off clusters, took them home and hosed them down.

The clams were less difficult. In knee-deep water, you had to push your foot down far into the mud and when you felt it bump into a clam, you went down and dug it up, immersing yourself in slick, gray mud.

Parents fail to understand why their kids play in mud. Could it be that they are preparing to find food when they grow up?

Maybe not but it works for me.

David and I soon were covered in the stuff, shivering but getting clams. At one point David, smeared in marsh mud, teeth chattering, looked at me and gave me a revelation.

"This is about as much fun as I can have," he said. We still agree on that.

The clams were called quahogs and they were big and useless for anything but chowder. Even at that you had to run them through a blender or chop them vigorously to reduce the pieces of meat to eat-able size.

David and I made our way south, down the marsh, boating what clams we could until the sky became darker. The wind got up in the north and was roughing the surface of the marsh.

We re-discovered the phenomenon that paddling a canoe upwind is inversely proportional to going the other way in terms of how much fun you are having.

After a half hour's labor and gaining less than 300 yards, we elected to leave the safety and warmth of the canoe and get back into the chilly, shallow water of the marsh and push the damned clams back to the boat ramp.

There were a few old boy fishermen standing around drinking beer and watching this with amusement. These guys had actual boats with motors and could have imagined that we were from the psychiatric hospital. They also had on dry clothes.

"That's the dock committee," said David.

I went to bed with a nasty cold that night but it was well earned.

OYSTER OR CLAM CHOWDER

The tools:
- Oyster knife
- Colander
- Cook's knife
- Can opener
- Cutting board
- 4-quart saucepan

Here's what you need from the store:
- 2 small sacks live clams or a pint of shucked oysters
- Butter / bacon / flour
- 1 tennis ball-sized onion
- Green onions & parsley
- Celery
- 1 red jalapeno chile
- Clam base (or chicken base)
- A can of creamed corn
- 1 small can of clam juice or a spoonful of clam base
- Milk
- Heavy cream
- Black, white & red pepper (cayenne)
- Paprika
- Tabasco

Here's how you put it together:

1. Put the bacon in the freezer 30 minutes ahead of time to firm it up then chop it into small pieces.

2. Strain the oysters and pick through them or steam open the clams and remove from the shells. Set aside.

3. Fry the chopped bacon in the saucepan until crispy.

4. Add 1 chopped onion, 1 rib chopped celery, 2 tennis ball sized red potatoes diced (skin-on is fine) and a half-bunch of chopped green onions.

5. Stir in a couple of spoons of flour.

6. Add the creamed corn and a handful of finely chopped parsley.

7. Add 1 mug of milk and 1 mug of heavy cream, stirring it in slowly.

8. Add a spoonful of clam or chicken base paste and blend.

9. Add the ground peppers. (You can add a little more milk if the mixture needs thinning).

10. Allow this to simmer for 15 minutes, then add the clams and a can of clam juice or the oysters.

11. Simmer for another 15 minutes.

12. Remove from the heat, cover and allow to stand for 5 minutes before serving. Sprinkle paprika or cayenne in the center of each serving.

Notes

FISHING BUDDY, JERRY COLLINS CELEBRATING WITH A BEER AFTER LANDING A 12-LB. BASS

Something Fishy

"The oyster being achieved, the next thing to be arranged for in the preparation of the world for man was fish. Fish and coal to fry it with."

– Mark Twain
"Was the World Made for Man?"

Fish, as every fifth grader knows, are a vital link in the earth's food chain. That is the primary function of fish and the office to which they have been assigned by Nature.

However, it seems likely that many people aren't aware of the second most significant reason for saltwater fish. I maintain (with apologies to Mark Twain) that it is to provide the key ingredient of court- bouillon. Only then, and as an afterthought; fried sea trout, pompano en papillote and stuffed flounder among other fishy masterpieces.

Whatever the true facts of the case, court bouillon remains one of the best reasons for the catching of fish in the first place and is certainly one of the best ways to enjoy their contribution to the food chain. Fortunately, you can find this out for yourself in the plan which follows.

Few things that you make at home better compliment an evening with people who enjoy each other's company than court bouillon.

It adapts well either to an elegant table or to sitting crosslegged on the floor with hand held chowder mugs.

GET FRESH AND MAKE A LOT!

The object is to get the freshest fish possible because fish can go bad quickly, even on ice. They contain a lot of fatty acids (the kind that are good for you); oily substances which are necessary for creatures who live in water which is often only a few degrees above freezing. You can use almost any fish you want, just make sure it's fresh.

Court bouillon is hard to make in small amounts so consider making it for a group of people, not just your date. It can be fun if you get your guests involved and participating in the process. Keep in mind that court bouillon takes about three hours, start to finish.

The plan which follows typically results in your having leftovers. This is good. The nice thing about court bouillon is that it is just as good the second day, if not better, even cold, straight out of the refrigerator. And with all those electrolytes swimming around in it, a world class "morning-after" cure and comfort.

A lot of hype used to surround the terms "blackened redfish" and "redfish court bouillon" but you don't need redfish to make court bouillon. Redfish and channel bass are the same thing. They are game fish, highly concentrated in shoreline waters from the mid-Atlantic coast around to Mexico. They became part of the Cajun craze that Chef Paul Prudhomme started in the 1980's, which almost wiped out the species. Chefs who didn't know any better insisted on including redfish in recipes – just like Chef Prudhomme insisted that you had to.

You can use almost any fish you want although I would not use monkfish or haddock. Salt water fish are best; for example red snapper, which really ARE red and not brown like redfish. Mako shark and catfish work, too. In fact, anybody with taste buds sufficiently educated to tell what kind of fish they are actually tasting in a court bouillon ought to will their taste buds to science.

COURT BOUILLON

The tools:

- Big pot (8-10 quart which you can buy at a restaurant supply store
- Cook's knife
- Cutting board
- Coffee mug/cup
- Garlic press
- Tablespoon
- Can opener

Here's what you need from the store:

- 4 pounds fresh fish fillets
- 2 big yellow onions
- Celery
- Clam base or chicken base
- 1 bunch green onions
- 4-5 jalapeno chiles
- Fresh parsley
- Garlic
- Dried bay leaves
- Peanut oil
- Flour
- Dried oregano
- Fresh basil
- Worcestershire sauce
- Red wine
- Tabasco
- Honey

Here's how you put it together:

1. Chop 2 onions, 4 stalks of celery, 1 bunch of green onions, 4 seeded jalapenos (or leave 2 with seeds), a half bunch of fresh parsley, a bunch of fresh basil and 5 or 6 cloves of garlic, smashed.

2. Pour a half coffee mug of peanut oil and a half cup of flour into the big pot and stir until golden color (you don't want a dark roux for this).

3. Add the cut up vegetables and fry on medium heat until tender (about 12 minutes).

4. Add half a jar of the clam or chicken base.

5. Add 4 quarts water.

6. Add half a bottle of red wine.

7. Add 4 or 5 dried bay leaves.

8. Add a small handful of the dried oregano.

9. Add two tablespoons of the worcestershire sauce.

10. Add two big spoonfuls of Tabasco.

11. Add a half a mug of honey.

12. Let this simmer for an hour, adjusting the thickness if needed by adding a little water. Let it cook down by about two inches.

13. Add the fish fillets cut into large pieces and allow to slowly simmer for 20 minutes.

14. Lay pieces of cooked fish in large, wide, bowls beside mounds of hot rice then spoon the courtbouillion over all.

(An)aerobic surf fishing

Bob Baringer and I were enjoying a gin and tonic on his screened porch. It was one of those pre-fall, Atlantic afternoons with lofty clouds over the beach and the smell of salt-borne on the remnants of the sea breeze.

The shadows of the clouds were making dark patterns on the water and you could easily imagine one of them to be a school of fish, moving slowly southward just a few hundred feet offshore. This was duly noted when we both realized that only one shadow was moving south. The others were moving east!

"What the hell is that?"

"It's a school," Bob hollered. You want to give it a shot?"

"Think we can make it?" I put down my glass.

"They're not in a hurry."

So we grabbed rods and reels, rigged them and sped over the dunes and down to the surf. On the first cast, we both got a fish.

We surged through the breaking waves back to the beach with our catch, dropped the fish in the sand and then ran south to get ahead of the school again. Once more into the surf; two casts, two fish, back to the beach and another run south.

At that point, we had four pan-sized Spanish mackerel weighing a couple of pounds each, randomly deposited in a 100-yard long line along the beach, marked by two sets of footprints.

"Another shot?"

We went back in and caught two more. I was ready to declare the fish the victors and wondering why I had ever put my glass down back at the porch.

With our gear and the remaining fish, we collapsed on the beach a few feet from the surf, where we lay on our backs, chests heaving for air, exhausted. There were beach strollers. They were staring. We had become tourist attractions. Maybe they thought we were just laughing ourselves to death for the hell of it, wheezing, sputtering, out of air and looking crazy. In such circumstances it is pointless to protest intelligence or to resist the consensus that you are completely nuts.

BARINGER WITH THE CATCH OF THE DAY

A simple way to cook fish

We filleted those mackerel, seasoned them with salt and pepper, shook them in some flour and sauteed them in a big chunk of butter in a skillet. Before taking them off the heat, a glass of chardonnay went into the pan and the juice of a half a lemon and the fish sizzled around in that for a few seconds.

I don't recommend using Spanish mackerel or bluefish for this because the filets are not good if they aren't very fresh and I mean fresh like same day as caught.

However, you can get tilapia fillets just about anywhere which will do fine if they're only "reasonably" fresh or if they're recently thawed. Most of the seafood at my store is thawed and works well enough. You can substitute lime for lemon. I don't use garlic for this because it can dominate the fish.

Almost any fish that is gently sauteed like this can become a little special if accompanied by a Crab Louis. Crab Louis, while being a salad, can easily second-string as an entree and if you add a potato, you've got supper.

The original plan for Crab Louis is thought by some to have originated in San Francisco or maybe Seattle, sometime around 1905 and was loosely based on a salad Nicoise which is much older and features tuna, not crab.

Nicoise ("neece-wahs") means "of Nice," the picturesque French city on the Mediterranean coast where Thomas Jefferson may long ago have been introduced to eggplant and macaroni.

Nice has a lengthy association with food. Archaeological evidence from the area indicates that people were making fire and cooking there 230,000 years ago, which is about 226,500 years before the Greeks invented Prometheus.

THIS IS A RED SNAPPER. IT IS *NOT* A REDFISH. A RED SNAPPER IS RED, A REDFISH IS BROWN.

CRAB LOUIS

The tools:

- 2-quart bowl
- Cutting board
- Cook's knife
- Tablespoon
- Coffee mug or measuring cup
- Glass container for refrigerator storage

Here's what you need from the store:

- Sour cream
- Mayonnaise
- Horseradish
- Tabasco
- Chili sauce (Heinz is the best)
- Green onions
- Parsley
- Lemon (big)
- 1-pound crabmeat cooked*
- 2 eggs
- 2 avocados
- 2 ripe tomatoes
- Iceberg lettuce

Here's how you put it together:

1. Stir the following into the bowl:

   Half-mug of sour cream

   Almost full mug of mayonnaise.

   1 tablespoon of horseradish

   2 finely chopped green onions

   3 or 4 sprigs finely chopped parsley

   6 or 8 shakes of Tabasco

   2 big tablespoons of chili sauce.

   Juice of half a big lemon

2. Fold in the crabmeat gently, so that you don't pulverize it.

3. After mixing, move the mixture to the small bowl, cover and refrigerate.

4. Peel and cut the 2 avocados and the 2 tomatoes into wedges.

5. Wash the leaves of the lettuce and dry them with paper towels.

6. Serve Crab Louis in mounds on plates of lettuce and garnish with slices of avocado, eggs and tomato.

*If you feel like splurging and have the coin, treat yourself to Jumbo Lump or King Crab meat.

If salad Nicoise actually is the idea behind crab Louis, then the Louis referred to in the name is probably Louis XIV, a world class gourmand. He really got into food, especially into oranges, then considered exotic. In fact, the first oranges in France came from his imported 100-year old orange tree. He built a special greenhouse for oranges called an "orangerie," near Versailles, which held 3,000 trees. Orangeries thus became status symbols for European royalty and still stand today on palace grounds from London to Moscow. You can thank old Louis, shown here all decked out for the painter, for leading to the manufacture of Cointreau, thereby contributing many years later to the refinement of cactus juice alcohol into the margarita that we know today.

Most things in life are not certain but here's one: Louis XIV never enjoyed fried catfish and hush puppies and probably didn't swill any homemade sweet iced tea, either. It's too bad because, being a gourmand, old Louis surely would have been charmed by a big basketful of hot, batter-dipped catfish and hushpuppies on a table draped in a brightly-colored, vinyl tablecloth with "Kiss Me, I'm Cajun" printed on it. He might even have approved of French fries and Dixie beer.

Catfish are not half as much fun to catch as they are to eat. If you catch them, you have to clean them and they are difficult to clean. Eating them, however, is as delightful as gritting up your face and your fingers with cornmeal crumbs and oil. It's hard to leave room for the hush puppies. Well, maybe not that hard.

FRIED CATFISH & HUSH PUPPIES

The supermarket will have all you need to make a great supper of catfish and hush puppies.

The tools:

- Cutting board
- Cook's knife
- Gallon Ziplock bag
- Big skillet
- Tongs
- 2-quart bowl
- Paper towels

Here's what you need from the store:

- Catfish fillets (allow 1 pound per person)
- Flour/eggs/cornmeal
- Peanut oil
- Salt & pepper
- Jalapeno chiles
- Green onions
- Eggs
- Peanut oil
- Onion
- Buttermilk
- Tabasco
- Salt & pepper

Here's how you put THE CATFISH together:

1. Season the catfish fillets with salt & pepper.
2. Combine a half-cup each of cornmeal and flour in a large ziplock bag.
3. Gently shake the fillets in the flour mix.
4. In a skillet, heat peanut oil 1-inch deep.
5. When oil is hot, lay the fillets in and fry on medium-high heat on both sides until golden.
6. Drain on paper towels and serve hot.

Here's how you put THE HUSHPUPPIES together:

1. In a bowl, mix 1 cup cornmeal with 3/4 cup flour, 1 teaspoon salt, 2 teaspoons baking powder, 1/2 teaspoon baking soda.
2. In a separate bowl, mix 1 large or jumbo egg with 3/4 cup buttermilk, 1/2 cup peanut oil, 1/2 very finely chopped onion, 3 very finely chopped green onions, 1 large, seeded very finely chopped jalapeno chile and/or some red pepper flakes.
3. Pour the liquid mix onto the dry mix and blend it in. Don't overdo the mixing.
4. Roll into balls and fry, 6 to 8 at a time until they are golden brown.

Drain on paper towels.

Notes: _____

_____

_____

_____

_____

_____

_____

_____

_____

_____

_____

_____

_____

_____

_____

_____

_____

_____

_____

_____

_____

_____

_____

_____

One of the joys of summer; from Judy's deck garden. Sweet and ready for picking

Salad days

Most of the plans in this book are written for you and your friends to have fun with in somebody's kitchen in lieu of eating out and spending a lot of money. Salads can help.

The one-dish meals, such as gumbo, court bouillon or lasagne need only the addition of a good salad and some hot bread to make a complete supper. A good salad is usually simple. Some are even inexpensive.

A few favorites are included here – along with plans for making homemade French dressing (which is quite different from store-bought), Roquefort dressing (with real Roquefort cheese) as well as my aunt Titter's favorite homemade mayonnaise, which she whipped up in her kitchen every few days.

FAVORITE GREEN SALAD

The tools:

- Cutting board
- Cook's knife
- Large bowl

Here's what you need from the store:

- Mixed spring salad greens
- Avocado
- Craisins or dried, sweet cranberries
- Jalapeno chiles
- Shelled pumpkin seeds
- Cucumber
- Cherry tomatoes or tomatoes
- Seedless baby tangerines
- Olive oil & balsamic vinegar
- Grated Romano cheese
- Fresh basil
- Optional: Garlic clove*

Here's how you put it together:

1. Rinse greens if necessary and dry in a salad dryer or drain well and roll up in a 4-foot length of paper towels until most of the loose water is gone.

2. In a large bowl put the greens, some fresh basil leaves, a few slices of avocado, a small handful of Craisins, a small handful of shelled pumpkin seeds, some cut-up tomato and cucumber.

3. Add a handful of fresh-grated Romano cheese and some black pepper.

4. Toss by hand with olive oil and a small amount of balsamic vinegar.

Useful tip: Rub the salad bowl with a halved, peeled garlic clove first.

THE SALT OF THE EARTH

Our word "salad" is from the Latin "salata" and the French "salade" both from the root "sal" or salt. Some believe that salad got its name from the fact that people ate salted greens prior to a meal, which the Romans were doing at least 1,600 years ago. Salt was a vastly more valuable commodity then than it is now, so when Roman soldiers got paid, they received their "salarium" or "salary," so that they could buy "sal" for their "salata." This also is the root for "salsa" and, because meats were pickled in salty brine, "souse" and thus "sauce" leading to "saucer" a plate for salads. Interestingly, the English word "silt" comes from the Danish "sylt" meaning the mud of a salt marsh.

CHECK YOUR PEDIGREE

Good olive oil (and bad olive oil) can come from practically any temperate place with low humidity and a lot of sunshine. Most of the world's supply is produced in Spain, followed by growers and mills in Italy, Greece, Tunisia and Syria. There are more than 200 olive oil producers in California.

In 2007, the UK Telegraph newspaper reported that only four percent of the olive oil exported from Italy is actually grown and pressed in Italy and that the country can not keep up with its domestic demand. There have been published reports of Italian oil misla-beling, resulting in some expensive "extra virgin olive oil" being too bitter to eat which had "imported from Italy" prominently on the label.

The term "extra virgin" signifies nothing more than "virgin" does all by itself. It's supposed to be the oil that has the lowest possible acidity (below 1%) and this typically is from the olives containing the most chlorophyll. You will see the term "first cold pressed" on some olive oil labels. You probably have some sort of vague understanding that this identifies the oil as being especially good or of the highest quality. However, the term "first cold pressed" means absolutely nothing and is used as a marketing ploy. There is no "second" press or "third" press and all olives are pressed at "room" or ambient temperature.

THE "WEDGE"

The tools:
- Cutting board
- Cook's knife
- Large bowl

CONDIMENTS PREPARED FOR TOPPING THE "WEDGE"

Here's what you need from the store:
- Two firm heads of iceberg lettuce
- A package of crumbled blue cheese or Roquefort cheese
- Mayonnaise
- Buttermilk
- Sour cream
- Tabasco
- Jalapeno chiles
- Shelled sunflower seeds
- Craisins
- Avocado
- Salt & pepper

Here's how you put it together:

1. About one hour before serving, fold together the following:
   - 1 cup mayonnaise
   - 1 cup buttermilk
   - 1 cup sour cream
   - 1 spoonful Tabasco
   - 1 package crumbled bleu cheese
   - Salt & pepper

2. Very finely chop the following:
   - 2 small seeded jalapeno chiles
   - 1 handful Craisins (or sweetened dried cranberries)
   - 1 handful sunflower seeds, walnuts, anything else you like.

3. Cut the lettuce into eight wedges.

4. Lay dollops of the cream mixture ver the wedges.

5. Top with the chopped condiments.

6. Serve with wedges of avocado.

THE WORSE IT SMELLS, THE BETTER IT TASTES

Blue/bleu cheese is good on practically anything, including salads. One of the best hamburgers made is smothered in melted Roquefort and cooked over a wood fire.

It is a member of a family of cheeses which have penicillin mold cultures added to them during production. These also are called simply "blue-green molds." The cheeses can be made from the milk of cows, sheep or goats and include Italian Gorgonzola, French Roquefort and English Stilton.*

The varieties, like most varieties of wine, are protected by designations of origin, so if you made Roquefort cheese in your own cave, you couldn't call it Roquefort officially or legally, even if your name was Roquefort and your cave was Roquefort Cave in Roquefort County, although nobody would put you in jail. I don't think.

You can use any of these cheeses in your salad dressing but the easiest probably is the packaged, already crumbled blue cheese.

* The so-called blue cheeses of various European cultures share a common characteristic. That the people of those cultures do not can be summarized by the following piece of irreverent profiling:

Heaven and Hell (author unknown)

"**Heaven** is where
The police are British
The cooks are French,
The workers are German,
The poets are Italian and
The administrators are Swiss.

Hell is where
The police are German,
The cooks are British,
The workers are French.
The poets are Swiss and
It's all run by the Italians."

HOMEMADE MAYONNAISE

Mayonnaise is thought to have originated on the island of Menorca, becoming popular in France in the mid-1700's. If you do this with a whisk, you'll need a team of two: one to whisk, the other to slowly pour the oil. Some plans call for olive oil but I don't recommend it because it makes the end result bitter tasting. A good vegetable oil will result in a sweeter mayonnaise.

The tools:

- 2 -quart bowl
- Electric mixer OR a whisk
- Tablespoon

Here's what you need from the store:

- Eggs
- Cider vinegar
- Coleman's dry English mustard
- 1 pint vegetable oil
- Paprika
- Salt

Here's how you put it together:

1. In a bowl mix three egg yolks with a tablespoon of vinegar, some salt, 1/2 teaspoon of dry mustard and a couple of taps of paprika.

2. While whisking steadily, slowly (very slowly) add the pint of vegetable oil. Try to "drizzle" it in so that it can properly emulsify. This should take a few minutes.

3. When the oil is all absorbed and the mixture is thick, remove the mayonnaise to another container and cover. Refrigerate before serving.

NOTE: You can do this by yourself, as I did for the photo below, but you will need to put the bowl on a wet, cloth towel on the counter top to keep it from sliding around and you will have to change hands frequently with the whisk.

I recommend a helper or else use an electric mixer on slow speed. The taste is worth it!

TOMATO ASPIC

The best foods to marginalize a hangover are Chinese leftovers, ice-cold buttermilk, cold soup, especially court bouillon and a good, chilled, homemade tomato aspic. You can load it with chopped celery, walnuts, shrimp, ripe avocado, citrus fruits, chopped olives, whatever suits you. Served on a bed of lettuce and topped with homemade mayonnaise, it is an elegant addition to put on any table.

The tools:

- Pot for boiling
- Ring mold or loaf pan

Here's what you need from the store:

- Gelatin (you'll use 4 envelopes)
- 1 big (46-ounce) can tomato juice
- Lemon
- Worcestershire sauce
- Celery salt
- Black pepper
- Tabasco (optional)

Here's how you put it together:

1. Put 4 envelopes of gelatin into a pot with 2 cups of the tomato juice and allow the gelatin to dissolve (about 10-15 minutes).

2. Place the pot on medium heat and add the juice of a large lemon, some salt and pepper, 2 tablespoons of worcestershire sauce, a spoonful of celery salt and a little Tabasco if desired.

3. Allow this to just barely come to a boil, stirring occasionally, then remove from the heat.

4. Pour into the ring mold and carefully refrigerate overnight.

NOTE: if you want a faster "set" to your aspic, fill the sink with ice and carefully nestle the aspic in the mold halfway into it without getting any water onto the aspic. Takes about an hour.

To release the aspic: Put a cold plate on top of the mold when the aspic is cold and has set. Turn mold and the plate over together. Put hot towels on the inverted mold for a few seconds to loosen then slide the mold up and off. Remove towels quickly. (You can always add but you can never subtract).

IMAGE COURTESY OF WWW.WHATSCOOKINGAMERICA.COM

SHRIMP SALAD

Shrimp salad is an easy lunch, a great summer side dish for supper or just a good reason to raid the icebox. It is especially good with homemade mayonnaise.

The tools:

- Pot for boiling shrimp
- Big bowl
- Big spoon
- Cutting board
- Cook's knife

Here's what you need from the store:

- One and a half pounds shrimp with the shells on
- Sweet pickle relish
- Black olives
- Water chestnuts (sliced)
- Zatarains Crab Boil
- Mayonnaise (unless you make it)
- Eggs
- Celery
- Tabasco
- Salt & pepper

Here's how you put it together:

1. Boil the shrimp in water with a box of Zatarains and a half-cup of salt for 10 minutes.

2. When cool, peel the shrimp and chop to desired size. (Don't rinse the shrimp).

3. Add the shrimp to the bowl and then add 3/4 cup mayonnaise, 1/2 cup chopped celery, a small handful of chopped black olives, 1/2 can sliced water chestnuts, a tablespoon of pickle relish, 2 chopped boiled eggs, Tabasco, salt & pepper as desired.

4. Mix well, cover and refrigerate until used.

Garnish with avocado slices, fresh tomato wedges, tangerine sections, whatever..

RICE AND TABASCO SALAD

This is a lot better than you might think.

The tools:

- Cutting board
- Cook's knife
- Large bowl
- Pot with a lid

Here's what you need from the store:

- Regular (not par-boiled) rice
- Tabasco
- Mayonnaise
- Water chestnuts, sliced
- Pine nuts
- Salt & pepper

Here's how you put it together:

1. Cook one cup raw rice in two cups of salted water.
2. When fully cooked*, place in a big bowl and allow to cool for 10 minutes.
3. Add 3/4 cup of mayonnaise.
4. Add 1 full Tablespoon of Tabasco or more.
5. Add a can of drained, sliced water chestnuts and some pine nuts.
6. Add some pepper and mix well. (Add more salt if needed).
7. Serve immediately while still warm or serve anytime chilled.

Remember to let the cooked rice steam in the pot for 10 minutes before taking the lid off.

BASIL / TOMATO ANTIPASTA

The tools:

- Flat serving dish with 1" sides
- Cutting board
- Cook's knife

Here's what you need from the store:

- 1 pound solid, whole milk mozzarella cheese, round pack
- Fresh basil
- Olive oil
- Red, ripe tomatoes
- Balsamic vinegar
- Salt & pepper

Here's how you put it together:

1. Slice the mozzarella into thin rounds.
2. Coat these slices in olive oil and lay them in the serving dish.
3. Cut a couple of tomatoes into thin slices and lightly season with salt & black pepper.
4. Tear some basil leaves and put this on the mozzarella
5. Drizzle olive oil on the tomato slices and then arrange them on the mozzarella slices.
6. Put more basil leaves on the tomatoes.
7. Repeat one more layer if desired.
8. Drizzle with a little of the balsamic vinegar (not much).

Serve at room temperature.

Potato Salad

It's advisable not to try making potato salad better by putting too much in it. Keep it simple and you'll have your guests wondering how you made potato salad taste so good. (Of course, if you like onions, mustard & bacon, by all means toss them in.)

The tools:

- Pot for boiling
- Colander
- Cook's knife
- Cutting board
- Big bowl

Here's what you need from the store:

- Medium red ("new") potatoes
- Sweet pickle relish
- Eggs
- Celery seed
- Mayonnaise (medium jar)
- Salt & paprika

Here's how you put it together:

1. Boil 6, tennis-ball sized potatoes on low for 30 minutes. Boil 4 eggs in the same pot for 10 minutes. Remove and cool. (Okay to leave the potato peel on if first washed).

2. Cut potatoes into half-inch cubes.

3. Put cut-up potatoes into a big bowl with half a jar of mayonnaise.

4. Cut up the boiled egg and add it in.

5. Add a third of a small jar of pickle relish (or about a quarter-cup).

6. Sprinkle in a spoonful of celery seed and mix this together. Season with salt to taste.

7. Mix well, garnish with a tap or two of paprika. Cover & chill.

"REAL" FRENCH DRESSING

It's a fancied-up vinaigrette. The French didn't invent it.

The tools:

- Cup or mug
- Teaspoon
- Tablespoon
- Garlic press
- Large jar with tight lid
- Mixing bowl

Here's what you need from the store:

- Sugar
- Peanut oil
- Ground cloves
- Worcestershire sauce
- Salt & pepper
- Cider vinegar
- Heinz chili sauce
- Onion powder
- Fresh garlic
- Lemon

Here's how you put it together:

1. Put 3/4 cup of sugar into the bowl.
2. Add 1 and a half cups peanut oil.
3. Add a Tablespoon of the worcestershire sauce.
4. Add 3 teaspoons salt.
5. Add a half-cup of vinegar.
6. Add a half-bottle of Heinz chili sauce.
7. Add some black pepper.
8. Add 2 cloves of garlic, smashed.
9. Whisk until well mixed then pour into the jar, seal and refrigerate overnight.
10. Before using, shake well.

Notes: _____

_____

_____

_____

_____

_____

_____

_____

_____

_____

_____

_____

_____

_____

_____

_____

_____

_____

_____

_____

_____

_____

_____

_____

_____

_____

_____

SWEETNESS & LIGHT!

Potables:
(FIVE OLD FAVORITES)

"The water was not fit to drink. To make it palatable we had to add whiskey. By diligent effort I learned to like it."

– Winston Churchill

Ramos Gin Fizz

The gin-based fizz (or "fiz" as it originally was spelled) became a favorite bar drink in New Orleans in the 1880's. The basic components are lime juice, lemon juice, sugar and egg white, shaken by hand with the gin, followed by a second shaking which includes the addition of crushed ice. If you add light cream and orange flower water, topped up with club soda at the end, you will have a Ramos gin fizz, so called because it was named after Henry Ramos, its inventor.

This drink is not good for a typical evening's libation because it requires a protracted amount of vigorous shaking – up to a minute or more. I have seen plans calling for a combined total of 12 minutes but that seems ridiculous.

In any case, if you drink two or three of them and then make a few for your guests, you may put in the equivalent of a light session at the gym, so that you can drink and get in shape at the same time.

Looked at solely from the standpoint practical gain, two of these give you most of your daily vitamin C requirement, provide you with a high level of cholesterol-free protein plus you get to shake off some calories just getting it into the glass.

However, from the perspective of taste, this wonderful, cold, frothy work of art is probably the most soothing pick-me-up you're likely to encounter after a long night's journey into day.

"Is this the way to Preservation Hall?"

My old boss, Dr. Floy Jack ("Flick") Moore hijacked me after dinner one evening in New Orleans, demanding that we hit at least one jazz club and that he buy me my first Ramos Gin Fizz. Our initial stop was the Napoleon House on Chartres Street in the Quarter, where we were served two, tall, frosted glasses of creamy refreshment and got to listen to Beethoven's *Eroica*, written by the composer for Napoleon.

An hour later we were still there, still listening to Beethoven and enjoying the fourth Ramos Gin Fizz as much as we had the first one. After a while, Flick remembered our commitment to jazz and we wandered off in search of it but didn't find it, returning to the Napoleon House just before they closed.

Must'a been the Beethoven

"Two Ramos Gin Fizzes, please," Flick told the white-aproned bartender.

"I'm sorry, sir, but there were two guys in here a while back drinking as many fizzes as we could shake and they completely wiped us out of cream."

Then they closed and we left the Quarter and walked across Canal Street and got breakfast and we never heard any jazz.

Ramos Gin Fizz

Apparently, there was a time in New Orleans when "shaker boys" were hired for the sole purpose of shaking drinks at the bar, particularly the Ramos Gin Fizz. When one boy wore out, the shaker was passed on to the next and so on, throughout the bar's busy times. No single bartender could do these things for a whole shift.

The tools:

- Cutting board
- Cook's knife or Bar knife
- Juicer
- Shaker
- Jigger (1.5 oz.)

Here's what you need from the store:

- Lemon & Lime
- Sugar
- Large Eggs
- Gin
- Orange flower water
- Light cream
- Vanilla extract

Here's how you put it together:

1. Into a tall bar glass put juice of 1/2 fresh squeezed lime and 1/2 fresh squeezed lemon.

2. Add 2 jiggers of simple syrup (1 part sugar to 1 part water).

3. Add 2 jiggers of gin.

4. Add 3 jiggers of cream.

5. Add the white of 1 large egg.

6. Add a half-jigger (no more!) of orange flower water.

7. Shake vigorously in a shaker for a minute

8. Add a big handful of ice and shake vigorously for another minute.

9. Strain into a collins glass. Top off with very cold club soda and a few drops of vanilla and stir gently.

You can buy orange flower water at gourmet shops or at amazon.com.

CLASSIC MARTINI

Dr. Fransiscus Sylvius, founder of the world's first academic chemical laboratory at Leiden University in Holland, in 1669, is credited with the invention of gin; a distillation of grain neutral spirits which was flavored by various botanicals, juniper being the most favored, then and now ("Gin" derives from "jenever," meaning "juniper." The word is not related to the Swiss city of Geneva.). It was thought to be medicine.

How nice it is nowadays to enjoy gin without having to get sick first!

The martini's obscure origin is claimed both by Martinez, California and by the Knickerbocker Hotel in New York. No one seems sure where the martini came from but the name itself apparently saw print first in the 1911 Bartender's Guide and that is probably ancient enough to establish a high pedigree.

During the liberation of Paris in 1944, Ernest Hemingway reportedly led a group of 50 combat irregulars into the Ritz Bar in Paris, "liberating" the famous old hotel from the fleeing Germans, who had used it as a headquarters. The barman, overcome with joy and excitement asked Hemingway what he would like and Hemingway is said to have answered "fifty-one dry martinis." If the legend isn't true, it should be.

A standard bar jigger holds an ounce and a half. Use that as follows:

CLASSIC MARTINI

1. A jigger of gin
2. Whatever part of a jigger of vermouth you prefer
3. Stir with a few cubes of ice and strain into a Martini glass or
4. Shake with a few cubes of ice and do the same.

Serve "up," garnished with an olive or a twist of lemon peel

Remember: without vermouth a Martini is just a glass of straight gin, which can make a good drink. It's just not a true Martini.

OLD FASHIONED

Good, old, American whiskey has a flavor often as much enjoyed when blended with something than when tasted straight. This propensity seems lacking in other forms of whiskey. Egg nog, for example, would be revolting if made with even the highest quality Scotch and yet an average American bourbon can make egg nog a cheery drink during the Christmas holidays.

The old fashioned, made with a little sweetness and a bit of Angostura bitters, can bring out the best in a good bourbon. When embellished with a bright cherry and a slice of orange, it becomes a friendly drink, indeed.

This drink seems rightly named since its first appearance reportedly was in the late 1800s, after having been identified as the first "cocktail" around 1806.

I was introduced to this famous concoction by old buddy, Bob Baringer, who came over to my house one evening and made up a mess of them to help me get over a cold. He is a licensed medical doctor and it was very satisfying to drink whiskey on doctor's orders! With the doctor!

It made the cold worse but I had too much fun trying to get "well" to care. There are several plans for the Old Fashioned. Here's one:

The Old Fashioned shares antiquity with the Sazerac Cocktail, which used Peychaud bitters instead of Angostura, among other things, and also claims the distinction of being the first cocktail invented. The Sazerac, native of the old Sazerac Hotel in New Orleans, currently has its official home at the Sazerac Bar in the Roosevelt Hotel on Barone Street near Canal and Bourbon Streets.

OLD FASHIONED

1. A jigger and a half of bourbon
2. A half jigger of simple syrup (equal parts water & sugar)
3. 2 dashes Angostura bitters
4. A twist of lemon peel (squeezed to liberate some oil)
5. A slice or wedge of orange
6. A maraschino cherry with stem (optional)

GIN & TONIC

By now, everybody knows that this hot weather favorite originated during the days of the British Raj, when soldiers serving in India were forced to take extract of Peruvian quinine to combat malaria. The quinine was extremely bitter tasting. To make it palatable, the troops in India cut it with sweetened soda water and called it tonic.

This still failed to measure up so the inventive chaps in the officers' corps added a healthy amount of gin and lime and instead of forcing it down with the troops every morning, started having it with their chums during the evening cocktail hour.

It quickly became the drink of an empire and has since remained a worldwide favorite.

Quinine was first produced by the Incas from the bark of quinquina tree. This process was taken over by the Spaniards, who reciprocated by nearly wiping the Incas out. Later on, world quinine production shifted to Indonesia but with the 1942 takeover of that nation by the Japanese, it became extremely hard to get. Science quickly devised a means of producing an artificial quinine and that is what today mostly is used in making tonic water.

In his book, *Islands in the Stream*, Hemingway tells you how to enhance a G&T with Angostura bitters. I tried it but didn't care for it. Here's the standard:

1. Fill a tall bar glass with ice.

2. Add a jigger of gin (well, maybe just a little more)

3. Fill the remainder with tonic water and, if you like, the juice of a lime wedge.

4. Garnish with a slice of lime.

I once asked a waiter in my hotel bar in Portugal for a gin and tonic and he returned with one in a glass containing no ice. I asked for ice. He stood as if dumbfounded for a moment then retreated behind the bar and placed one ice cube in an empty ice bucket with silver tongs, brought the bucket to my table and with great flourish, dropped that lonely cube ceremoniously into my glass.

DAIQUIRI

The original permutation of what we now variously call the daiquiri is attributed to a bar near a beach in Santiago, Cuba around the turn of the last century. It reportedly was limited to sugar, lime juice and rum.

Subsequent translations of the recipe insisted on lemon juice, the overcoming of which error may be one explanation behind such versions as the strawberry daiquiri, the melon daiquiri and the avocado daiquiri.

Probably the most storied daiquiri in the world is the one invented in 1932, by the legendary Havana bartender, Constantino Ribalaigua, for the world's most emulated and deified barfly, Ernest Hemingway. He named it "El Floridita Number Three." Hemingway liked his drinks unsweet and the "number three" meets that qualification.

The famous writer had his own designated stool in the La Floridita Bar (which Ribalaigua owned) and he would appear there in the mornings to read his newspaper and to drink the "Papa Doble"; a "Number Three" times two (you do the math) which the author is said to have been a great help to the deft and talented Ribalaigua in creating, assuming he needed any help.

Today the famous barstool is graced by a statue of Hemingway. On the wall behind it is a picture of the writer chatting with the fatigues-clad Fidel Castro, following a fishing tournament which the non-fisherman Castro, of course, "won."

Hemingway, an earnest champion of the left, was likely not as enthusiastic about totalitarianism and despotic dictators as some airhead notables are today. Nevertheless, Castro blatantly chummed up to him in front of the cameras. That was good, if somewhat shameless, P.R. That was also before the dictator stole the deceased Hemingway's property in Cuba in the name of the revolution which now egregiously honors his erstwhile bar presence with this ridiculous statue. The following is as close as you are likely to get to the original "Papa doble."

ERNEST HEMINGWAY AND FIDEL CASTRO
PRINTED FROM: HTTP://WWW.LIFE.COM/IMAGE/FIRST/IN-
GALLERY/22999/CASTRO-REVOLUTIONARY-AS-CELEBRITY
© 2011 SEE YOUR WORLD LLC. ALL RIGHTS RESERVED

THE PAPA DOBLE DAQUIRI

THE "PAPA DOBLE"; SHAKEN & STRAINED, WITH PLENTY OF FRESH GRAPEFRUIT & LIME JUICE

1. 3 oz white rum

2. 1.5 oz. fresh lime juice (or a half of a lime)

3. ½ oz. fresh grapefruit juice (or a lot more; see note below)*

4. 1.5 oz. maraschino liqueur (or 1/2 oz. pomegranate liqueur)

5. 1 cup shaved ice (or a handful of ice cubes)

6. Process by vigorously by shaking with a cup of shaved ice between two cocktail shakers until the drink is foamy. Strain and serve "up" in a cocktail glass.

Any sweetness the drink has comes from the grapefruit and the maraschino liqueur but it isn't much. Maraschino liqueur is a clear substance, made from sour marasca cherries grown in Croatia and aged for two years in wooden casks. The result is totally unlike the over-sweet maraschino cherries used to accent old fashioneds and various paper-umbrella drinks. Do not use lemon or sugar if you want the authentic "El Floridita Number Three."

*(This excellent drink is equally tasty, in my opinion, when made with pomegranate liqueur instead of maraschino liqueur. They both are tart . **Use the juice of one-fourth to one half of a fresh grapefruit** and shake the drink vigorously between a tall glass and a shaker with four or five cubes of ice until its real cold and foamy. Then strain it into a martini glass. You may prefer Mount Gay "silver" rum to Bacardi and if you use two ounces, not three, you can enjoy more than one. Or two.*

"Constante, is this the number four or the number six?"

There are several plans for this "Hemingway Daiquiri" and they are different. You may wonder if Hemingway himself wrote down successive versions of Constantino's original recipe while sitting there on his designated stool at the front corner of the bar. In that case, the recipe may have well have changed incrementally with each daiquiri Hemingway dispatched, sort of like rewriting the ending of *The Sun Also Rises* numerous times. Hemingway is variously reputed to have consumed 6 or maybe 7 or even 16 "Papa Dobles" at a sitting, so it is little wonder that the plan could have morphed over a morning's refreshment.

If you actually *were* to drink 16 of these in a row, you would consume 48 ounces of white rum, which is exactly three pints. This sounds suspiciously concocted as another part of Hemingway's "I-can-drink-you-under-the-table" legend.

It doesn't help that freelance mixologists have jumped in over the years with their own versions, so that the ingredients, the proportions and the methods are as different from each other as they are from Ribalaigua's original. One of Hemingway's own versions calls for *the juice of a half a grapefruit*. (This is really good!).

"El Floridita number three" is better if shaken in shaved ice and strained than it is if processed in a blender. Many drinkers might find it lacking in sweetness. I don't but it may explain why most daiquiri recipes call for sugar, simple syrup or a sweet component such as grenadine. I strongly advise the complete avoidance of simple syrup, sugar or any sweetener! Go with the lime and grapefruit.

ERNESTO AT THE WHEEL OF PILAR

For a pitcher of these, make the batch size small, probably not more than triple the above plan. Of course it's just a drink so who cares what's in it as long as you like it? A bunch of us were back in the kitchen at the old Florida beach house one night and decided to take additional liberties with the daiquiri concept. We came up with the following:

1. A blender half-full of crushed ice or ice cubes,
2. A large handful of freshly picked mint leaves, stems removed,
3. A quarter-can of Minute Maid frozen limeade, large can, undiluted,
4. 2 jiggers (3 or 4 ounces) gin or white rum,
5. Then blend until the contents become a brilliant, green slush.
6. Serve in cocktail or martini glasses.

Considering the fact that anybody, anywhere contemplates making an avocado daiquiri, a banana daiquiri or a coconut daiquiri, there should be no reason to feel embarrassed by the disapproving stares of would-be daiquiri purists when you enjoy your mint "daiquiri."

I wish we had thought at the time to give it a name.

Elbow to elbow, no television

Hemingway liked drinking and did it well. If it interfered with his writing you never suspected it. He not only drank well, he wrote well about drinking. In those passages in his books where he describes a drink in detail, you have to fight the urge to put the book down and go into the kitchen and make one for yourself. One imagines he would have been a hell of a fine contender to rub elbows with at the bar.

In fact, Hemingway, at about the age of 50, would seem an excellent first choice to be the one standing next to you at the bar in that part of Heaven set aside for such imperfect worthies as the writer himself and you and I.

"Betcha can't eat just four . . ."

Mornings After

OLD FRIEND DAVID HACKNEY CAUGHT MAKING BREAKFAST

*"He that looketh on a plate of ham and eggs to lust after
it hath already committed breakfast with it in his heart."*

– C.S. Lewis.

Remember those camping trips when you were in the Scouts and tried to make pancakes in the woods in the morning over a campfire? With a folding and well-dented aluminum mess kit?

You would be cold and your arm would shake and your aluminum mess kit pan would tilt and the batter would follow gravity to the low end.

The smoke got into your eyes no matter which point of the compass you chose to hunker down on. The smoke was a problem because it kept you from opening your eyes and seeing the little flakes of ash that rose out of the burning sticks and curled around your aluminum mess kit pan and fell into your slowly migrating batter thereby seasoning your hoped-for pancakes with crunchy, oxidized oak or hickory.

You and your pals called them "scrambled pancakes" because the aluminum mess kit pan was designed to cling to anything the same way velcro does and you had to scrape them up and turn them over in broken sections.

Goodness gracious they were good!

By the time you did two of them, the first was already cold and when you finally had what you euphemistically called a "stack" those on the bottom had got stuck to the plate from the cold. It didn't matter. You had rarely been that hungry and so they were a joy to eat, swimming in puddles of cold syrup, ashes and all.

HALF & HALF PANCAKES*

Keep your pancakes warm in the oven with the temperature set at 210 degrees.

The tools:
- Bowl
- Whisk
- Large spoon
- Skillet or griddle
- Spatula (flipper)
- Paper towels

Can be made with buttermilk if you prefer.
Use buttermilk OR half & half, but not both.

Here's what you need from the store:
- All purpose flour
- Eggs
- Peanut oil & paper towels
- Butter
- Half & Half
- Baking powder
- Baking soda
- Sugar (or sweetener) & syrup
- Salt

Here's how you put it together:

1. Put a cup and a half of flour In the bowl.
2. Add one tablespoon of baking powder.
3. Add half spoonful of salt.
4. Add half a small spoonful of baking soda.
5. Add a big spoonful of sugar.
6. With a whisk, blend all the dry stuff.
7. In the other bowl, pour two cups of half of the half & half. (Add more if needed).
8. Add two fresh regular eggs (or one jumbo egg).
9. Add a quarter cup of peanut oil.
10. Beat this with a whisk just until blended*.
11. Pour some oil on the skillet and wipe off the excess with a paper towel.
12. Pour the batter onto the hot skillet or griddle until it forms a circle as big as you want your pancake to be.
13. When the top gets "holes" from bubbles in the batter, turn your pancake over and allow it to cook the same amount of time. Note: If the batter starts to lump up or look odd, rewhisk.

BUTTERMILK BISCUITS

Serves 6

The tools

- Cutting board
- A bowl
- Whisk
- Tablespoon
- Teaspoon
- Hand-held dough knife (u-shaped, multi-blade)
- Mug or cup
- Non-stick aluminum foil
- Oven cookie sheet pan

Here's what you need from the store:

- All purpose flour
- Shortening or butter
- Buttermilk
- Baking powder
- Baking soda
- Salt

Here's how you put it together:

1. Preheat oven to 400 degrees.
2. Put a cup and a half of flour In the bowl.
3. Add a big spoonful of baking powder.
4. Add half a small spoonful of salt.
5. Add half a small spoonful of baking soda.
6. With a whisk, blend all the dry stuff.
7. Using the dough knife, "Cut in" a -stick of cold, unsalted butter or cold shortening until the whole thing is "grainy" looking.
8. Pour in a little buttermilk and blend it in with a large spoon. Keep pouring in a little at a time until the mixture is soft and pliable but not too wet and sticky. (if it gets too wet, add a little more flour).
9. Toss a small handful of dry flour into the bowl so that it coats the ball of mix.
10. Roll the bowl around a couple of times to loosen the ball. Or use a rubber spatula).
11. Dump the mix out onto a floured cutting board.
12. With a floured rolling pin (or wine bottle) press out the dough until it is about 3/4 inch thick.
13. Fold this over on itself and press gently and repeat 5 or 6 times then roll it out on the board again.
14. Cut the flat dough into rounds with a wine glass or whatever you have.
15. Lay the raw biscuits on a sheet of no-stick aluminum foil on a cookie sheet and brush the tops with some melted butter.
16. Bake for about 18 to 20 minutes or until the tops are golden brown.

Huevos Rancheros

If you never had these, you are in for a treat. And if you've had them in restaurants, the same applies. It's well worth the extra trouble to chop and blend your own salsa rather than to use the store-bought kind. The commercial version is convenient but so is instant coffee. You should be able to make a good salsa in less than five minutes if you spend the first minute getting everything laid out, lined up and in place.

This goes well with a few links of smoked sausage and double-strength coffee with brown sugar and half & half. I should add that if you are sensitive to raw onion you can leave it out and still have a good salsa.

HUEVOS RANCHEROS

Serves 2

The tools:

- Cutting board
- Cook's knife
- Bowl
- Skillet
- Plate for warming

Make your salsa by hand on the cutting board. Using a food processor turns it all into a kind of relish. Make this just before serving for the ultimate freshness.

Here's what you need from the store:

- 2 fresh, ripe tomatoes
- 2 fresh jalapenos
- Fresh cilantro
- Green onions
- 1 small sweet (Vidalia) onion
- 1 or 2 avocados
- 1 can refried beans
- Eggs
- Soft corn tortillas
- Ground cumin
- Chili powder
- Olive oil
- Butter
- Salt & black pepper
- Tabasco
- Lime

Here's how you put it together:

1. *Make the salsa:* finely chop the jalapenos, tomatoes, the onion, two green onions and a small amount of chopped, fresh cilantro, and blend it in a bowl with a little salt, black pepper, cumin, chili powder and Tabasco.

2. Fry 4 tortillas in some butter and olive oil on both sides and keep on a warming plate in an oven set at 130 degrees.

3. Fry the number of eggs you want, (over lightly or sunny side up).

4. Plate the tortillas on warm plates and spread each on one side with a thin coat of the refried beans.

5. Lay the eggs on the tortillas and then quickly fry the salsa for 30 seconds in the skillet, just enough to warm slightly.

6. Spoon the salsa over the eggs and serve garnished with avocado slices. Add a few splashes of lime and Tabasco.

GRITS

Back in my youthful newspaper days I would occasionally be a smart-ass and write hoaxes for the amusement of both unsuspecting and savvy readers. I always said they were hoaxes but it didn't matter. Some people took them hook, line and sinker.

The one that haunts me to this day is the column in which I went into some detail revealing for my northern readers how grits were harvested from "grits trees." The report pointed out how large tarps were laid out underneath the trees at harvest time and how tractors with big vise grips on the front would grab the trees and shake them vigorously, causing the grits to fall onto the tarps. I received some letters from people thanking me for clearing up a mystery and others angrily pointing out that I was a smart-ass and should go get a real job. Maybe on a farm, growing corn.

Oh, well.

You can't get decent grits in restaurants anymore. Sadly, you can't get any kind of grits in most restaurants. The good news is you can make your own.

I strongly recommend fresh, stone ground grits but they're almost impossible to find today. However, there is a source that grinds daily and they will ship them to you fresh off the stone mill. They are probably the best you're likely to find:

OAKVIEW FARMS GRANARY
164 DEWBERRY TRAIL
WETUMPKA, AL 36093
334-567-9221
www.oakviewfarms.com

These (but not all) grits require a ratio of three-to-one, water to grits. Bring the water to a boil then reduce heat and whisk the grits in. Stir. Start them slow, cover the pot, cook them slow with plenty of butter and salt, stir every few minutes. After 25 minutes remove from the heat cover and allow to stand for 3 or 4 minutes before serving. If you like the rich corn flavor of popcorn, you'll love these. Try crumbling some crispy bacon in them at breakfast.

And save the sugar for the oatmeal!

OATMEAL

Porridge, or a mixture of legumes or grains cooked in water, stock or other liquid, has been a staple for thousands of years. Socrates and Plato may well have enjoyed a bowl on the sunny streets of Athens before resuming their morning's work of corrupting local youths. In England, a coarse mixture of cooked peas would be eaten for several subsequent days, thus giving us the nursery rhyme "Pease porridge hot, pease porridge cold" which apparently were consumed "in the pot, nine days old." And this was before refrigerators!

One may wonder if three days might have been enough. Or two.

To many, the best porridge to eat all by itself is oatmeal. The problem is that a lot of people don't know how to make oatmeal or else imagine that it is too much trouble to go to in the first place.

But you can do this:

Oatmeal is something anybody can do because it is very forgiving even if you don't measure stuff. All you have to do is boil it down until it gets thick then put a lid on the pot and let it stand for a few minutes.

Try this:
1. Put some water in a pot (not a huge pot, just a regular old pot that has a lid). How much water? Let's say two cups.
2. Add some salt and a pat of butter and bring it to a boil.
3. When it's boiling, dump in some oatmeal. How much oatmeal? Let's say almost a cup of the "quick" (but NOT instant!) rolled oats type.
4. After about five minutes, when the porridge has thickened, put the top on the pot and remove it from the heat. Allow this to sit undisturbed for about five minutes (this allows the oatmeal to "set" and not to be runny).
5. In the bowl, add whatever fruit you like (or none) and some sugar (or none) and a little half & half (or none).

Of course, you may want to follow the instructions on the package but I just wing it as per above.

Oatmeal not only is delicious, it is one of the most nutritious cereal grains available. Oats contain fiber that dissolves in water, so that this fiber is absorbed into the blood stream and stabilizes the absorption of glucose thus helping to maintain optimal blood sugar levels. It also reduces cholesterol in the body naturally.

You can buy other types of oatmeal. Try Scottish oatmeal and steel cut oats, both packaged by Bob's Red Barn company. (*That's another Bob*).

MUFFINS

The good thing about muffins is that they are not much harder than waking up and going into the kitchen. I have found that if you try to follow "recipes" for muffins you can wind up making them difficult. They are not difficult. Here's my formula, worked out through trial & error:

- You need three cups of dry stuff, give or take.
- You need some salt, baking powder and sugar or sweetener
- You need a couple of eggs and about 3/4 stick of butter.
- You need two cups of some kind of liquid which can include fruit puree.

For example:

In the "dry" bowl put a cup of "King Arthur" whole wheat flour, a cup of wheat bran, a cup of dry oatmeal, 1 Tablespoon of baking powder, a half teaspoon of salt, a quarter-cup of brown sugar (or more), some chopped nuts and/or raisins if you like.

In the "wet" bowl put two smashed or pureed very ripe bananas, 3/4 stick of butter (melted) , two jumbo eggs, 1/2 cup half & half and blend well.

Pour the wet stuff on top of the dry stuff and blend it all well. Then put the mix into your greased muffin tins (almost to the top) and bake in an oven preheated to 350 degrees for 25 minutes. I use the large size muffin tins. *You can also buy paper muffin cups and reduce clean up problems almost completely.* You can replace some of the bananas with apple sauce.

This will make about 8 large muffins. They are good for a couple of days if you let them cool completely at room temperature then put them in something and keep them in the refrigerator.

Muffins are good with softened cream cheese. You can add raisins, walnuts, dried cranberries, blueberries, whatever. For corn-bread muffins use 1 + 3/4 cup cornmeal, 1/2 cup flour, 1/2 teaspoon salt, 4 teaspoons baking powder, 1/2 teaspoon baking soda, 1+3/4 cups buttermilk, 2 eggs and a stick of butter (melted). Bake at 425 degrees for 20 minutes.

CRUNCHY FRENCH TOAST
Serves 2

The tools:

- Whisk
- Ziplock bag
- Skillet
- Casserole dish
- 2 plates

Here's what you need from the store:

- Bread (Italian bread pictured)
- Eggs
- Butter
- corn flakes
- milk
- Cinnamon
- Syrup

Here's how you put it together:

1. Crush corn flakes, using a rolling pin or wine bottle) in a ziplock and spread on a plate.

2. In a flat casserole dish, whisk 6 eggs and a small amount of salt & milk.

3. Dip the bread slices in the egg (both sides) then coat with the crushed corn flakes.

4. Fry both sides in butter on medium heat until golden. Plate the finished slices and place oven set to 130 degrees to keep warm.

5. Dust with a little cinnamon.

6. Top with your choice of fruit or serve with syrup.

Many years ago, before trans fat, before eggs became bad for you or chocolate became good for you, or before butter was bad for you and then became good for you again, there was a kid's show on every Saturday morning called "Mister Wizard" in which a nice man would show bright but ignorant kids neat stuff about science. I have long forgot any of the shows' content but I do remember the sponsor's punch line during the commercials. It told kids what made a good breakfast; fruit, cereal, milk, bread and butter.

Crunchy French Toast can include all five of those things plus eggs so that your kids can eat what you think is junk and they'll still be getting a healthy, reasonably well balanced breakfast.

Eggs Sardou

Here's another French-Creole creation of the famous Antoine's Restaurant in New Orleans. This one is well over 100 years old. It has nourished breakfast and brunch patrons over the span of those years, becoming a famous old favorite.

It makes an elegant brunch. It takes time and some care and, like most things, is most efficiently made when all of the tools and ingredients are arranged for use ahead of time.

Poached Eggs

Into simmering water 3" deep in a big skillet, place 4 to 6 eggs. It's advisable to crack the eggs into small, separate cups first then very gently "roll" them out into the water. Don't let the water boil but keep it pretty hot. To avoid the whites from becoming stringy, add a couple of teaspoons of vinegar to the water. Cook about 3 minutes, less if you like really runny eggs. Or just use an egg poacher.

EGGS SARDOU
allow 2 eggs and 2 artichoke bottoms per person

This can be an excellent team project. The bechamel (white) and Hollandaise sauces can be farmed out individually while another cooks the spinach and poaches the eggs. Eggs Sardou is good with a hot, French baguette and a light, refreshing wine, such as my favorites, ice cold vinho verde or a crisp champagne. Another great compliment is the original Ramos Gin Fizz, which is featured in the previous section (page 159).

The tools:

- Whisk
- Egg poacher (optional)
- Skillet or Dutch oven
- Double boiler (or makeshift)

Here's what you need from the store:

- Lemons
- Eggs
- Artichoke bottoms (canned)
- Heavy cream
- Butter
- Wine vinegar
- Spinach
- Flour
- Nutmeg
- Cayenne pepper
- Tabasco
- Worcestershire sauce
- Paprika

Here's how you put it together:

1. Make a sauce as follows: 1/4 stick of butter melted in a pan. Add a heaping regular spoonful of flour and whisk until nice & bubbly. Add 10 ounces heavy cream slowly, whisking until smooth. Remove and set aside (keep warm)

2. Mix 1 cupful of chopped cooked and pressed dry spinach with the sauce and a dash of nutmeg.

3. Go back to page 45 and make the bearnaise sauce without any tarragon, and call it a Hollandaise sauce.

4. Divide the creamed spinach equally onto warmed plates.

5. Top each mound with an artichoke bottom or two.

6. Place a poached egg on each artichoke bottom.

7. Smother this with warm Hollandaise sauce and garnish with a little paprika or cayenne pepper.

"Save room!"

KEY LIME PIE WITH WHIPPED CREAM

Our dad was not a cook. Those talents were taken in the family by his sister, who could have cooked a two-by-four if you gave her enough onions and butter. Dad produced only two things in our kitchen: a very heavy, dark, chocolate pie and a meaty, red, spaghetti sauce. He did one or the other when the mood struck, usually on a rainy Sunday afternoon.

He loved adding new things to his spaghetti sauce, like pecans or water chestnuts and I can testify that it was rarely the same sauce as the one he did the time before. It was unfailingly good. We loved it.

Dad's spaghetti was my introduction to making food without engineering it, thus killing the fun. He had fun. On those Sunday afternoons he liked to pour a small glass of whiskey for himself and launch into the uncharted territory of "let's try some of this and see what happens."

This kind of cooking is user-friendly. It is also people-friendly and you will find, if you haven't already, that getting a good feast together with all hands on deck in the kitchen is a great way to bond friendships. And if you screw something up, well, you will have learned something. Besides, what you learn from success seldom surpasses what you learn from failure.

Dad's Chocolate Pie

To do this flourless dessert the way he did, pour yourself a small glass of good whiskey and sip it so that it's all gone just when it goes into the oven. A good Scotch will work. This won't guarantee success but Dad practiced it to keep failure from being unpleasant, should it occur.

The tools:

- Whisk
- Double boiler (or makeshift)
- A mug or measuring cup
- Big spoon
- 9-inch round cake pan

Here's what you need from the store:

- Baker's semi-sweet baking chocolate
- Sugar
- Salt
- Eggs
- Light cream
- Vanilla
- Butter

Here's how you put it together:

1. Preheat oven to 300 degrees.

2. Grease & flour the inside of a 9" pie pan.

3. Separate enough eggs to have 5 ounces of egg yolks (save the whites for omelets*, and other purposes).

4. In a double boiler over low heat, put 5 ounces of butter, 5 ounces semi-sweet Baker's chocolate, 5 ounces sugar and when it's all melted, whisk in the 5 ounces of egg yolks and 5 ounces of light cream. When smooth and creamy, pour into the prepared pie pan and bake at 300 degrees for 32 minutes. Let stand to cool then refrigerate before serving cold.

SERVE THIS STRAIGHT FROM THE REFRIGERATOR

SOUTHERN PECAN PIE

The tools:
- 2-quart pot
- Whisk
- Mug
- Bowl

Here's what you need from the store:
- Enough pecans to fill 3 cups (or more)
- 1 bottle clear Karo corn syrup
- Vanilla extract
- Butter
- Eggs
- 2 frozen pastry pie shells
- Salt

Here's how you put it together:

1. Pour one, 16-ounce bottle of Karo syrup into the pot with the heat on medium.
2. Add a big mugful of white sugar and stir with the whisk until the sugar has almost dissolved. Remove from heat.
3. Add a stick of butter and blend well.
4. Beat 6 jumbo or extra large eggs in a bowl with just a little salt and whisk them in.
5. Add a tablespoon of vanilla extract.
6. Add 3 or 4 big handsful of pecans, stir and pour into the pie shells.
7. Bake at 330 degrees for 65 minutes.

Pecans are one of the few foods indigenous to North America. The nut was a favorite of native Americans and was cultivated by Americans long before the Revolutionary War. None other than Thomas Jefferson himself planted pecan trees at Monticello. George Washington grew them at Mount Vernon after Jefferson gave him some young pecan saplings.

Thus, you can make the case that pecan pie is vastly more American than apple pie, apples being native to Europe and Asia.

The key to a good pecan pie is oven time. The custard part of the pie has to caramelize and you can't do that in a hurry. Frozen pastry shells are packed in twos so the following makes two pies as they freeze well.

You can buy some of the best pecans available in the U.S. from the Orangeburg Pecan Company in South Carolina at www.uspecans.com.

"AS AMERICAN AS PECAN PIE!"

KEY LIME PIE

The tools:

- 2-quart pot
- Whisk
- Mug
- Bowl
- Citrus juicier
- Food grater

Here's what you need from the store:

- 6 limes (thin skinned are jucier)
- 1 can (14-oz.) sweetened condensed milk
- Eggs
- Prepared graham cracker pie shell

Here's how you put it together:

1. Put one can of condensed milk in a bowl.

2. Add the yolks of 6 large eggs and blend with a whisk.

3. Add a half-mug of fresh squeezed lime juice.

4. With the "sawtooth" part of the grater, grate about a tablespoon of lime zest from the peel, being careful not to get any of the white, and add it to the bowl.

5. Pour this mixture into a 9-inch pie shell and bake 14 minutes in a preheated oven at 350 degrees.

6. Cool then refrigerate. Top with whipped cream.

The key lime is the same lime as the Mexican lime. It was brought to the Caribbean by the Spanish in the 16th Century and today it is common throughout the region as well as in Mexico and Southern Florida. The skin is yellow when ripe and the fruit is smaller than the deep green Persian limes you are likely to encounter in the store.

However, Persian limes are fine to use for making key lime pie if you can't get any of the true key limes. Avoid using bottled lime juice or food color.

Mexican limes are native to Malaysia. They grow on small, thorny trees. Most of the limes produced commercially come from Mexico and are Persian or Tahitian limes. The true key lime is less hardy and more difficult to grow and to harvest but they are worth the effort to find.

When you ask for "lemon" in Mexico, you are going to get a lime, which they call "limon," which is why lemons mistakenly got included into daiquiris.

DRUNK BANANAS

If you forget dessert until the last minute and happen to have some sherry and a few bananas lying around, this can be a worthy last-minute improvisation. Ice cream helps, too. It's a lazy man's version of bananas Foster but there is little risk that it will overtake that famous dessert in popularity.

All you do is cut up as many bananas as you think you need, toss the slices in a heated skillet with a good amount of butter, sprinkle some brown sugar or regular sugar on top, let it bubble around in there for a minute and then pour in a couple of jiggers of sherry. Serve with ice cream or whipped cream on top, maybe with a pinch of cinnamon or nutmeg and some chopped nuts. I sometimes add a jigger of cognac to the sherry.

Suggestion: always have some sherry or cognac in the cupboard, some bananas in the fruit bin and some ice cream in the freezer. You can also substitute peaches, mangoes or apples with cinnamon for the bananas and if you never make any dessert, you can drink the sherry and the cognac.

The original Bananas Foster was invented at Brennan's Restaurant in New Orleans in 1951, by chef Paul Blange. The "Foster" in the name was Richard Foster, a friend of restaurant owner Owen Brennan. Brennan's estimates that 35,000 pounds of bananas are used every year to make Bananas Foster, one of the restaurant's most popular menu items. You can easily get Brennan's famous recipe for this by visiting their website at **www. brennansneworleans.com.**

In Retrospect

The drawbacks to making great food are that it takes time and money and you have to be focused. This also applies to great sex but people go ahead and do it anyway, despite the costs and distractions.

A lot of us would like to try our latent talents in the kitchen but get "performance anxiety" and say to hell with it and just stick to grilling steaks or making drinks.

Every man and woman can cook well if encouraged. Cookbooks typically are not encouraging and some are even intimidating. Most certified chefs share the manly traits of never asking anybody for directions and seldom measuring anything. which is the mandate of most cookbooks. Making great food is an adventure! Men like adventure even if it means driving past a gas station against the wise advice of a female in the passenger seat.

I realize that measuring is the only sure way to replicate the things we cook so that they resemble the original. However, there are too many minute differences in the end results to achieve exactness. So there are times when "some" cayenne pepper is better than "1/4 teaspoon." Let it be a judgement call. If you have to worry about a quarter-teaspoon my advice is get somebody else to cook.

These pages include plans to enable the novice to make a few great dishes and tell where they originated. I spent a few years as a novice, so I know how it feels when you plate up your first big supper for your date and your friends. So, believe me, you can do this!

By now I trust you have found that your own good food brings a lot to friendly gatherings. Even a few unfriendly gatherings can be made tolerable by the addition of a great gumbo or a hot lasagne and a good food story or two. By making the things in here you will develop your own, unique skills and be able to launch your own plans.

Many years ago, there used to be a cartoon advertisement printed on the back cover of magazines and comic books which read: "THEY LAUGHED WHEN I SAT DOWN TO PLAY THE PIANO." The ad showed how an ordinary klutz took the piano lessons being hawked and became an accomplished virtuoso in front of his friends. This book won't enable you to play the piano or even whistle "Dixie" but it will help you turn out some really good food.

It also might inspire your friends not to laugh when you tell them you're going to make their supper.

Then, when they see you are serious, give them a glass of wine, a knife, a cutting board, something to chop and a little supervision and enjoy the result.

And the food.

About the Author

Bob Cotten left newspaper reporting in the South to spend the next 15 years writing and directing documentary films and television science programs. He later followed his taste buds to create Bob Cotten Gourmet Specialties, serving 20 years as the company's recipe developer and chief promoter in the eastern U.S. and in Europe. He shared his kitchen talents in a humorous newspaper column entitled "Bachelor Cook," written mostly for people wanted to cook but were intimidated by all the minutiae. He now lives with his wife, Judy, in eastern Pennsylvania.

Index

South on a Plate
Publications

21 Northridge Drive West
P.O. Box 13
Mohnton, PA 19540

7613486R0

Made in the USA
Charleston, SC
23 March 2011